The Marshmallow fluff Cookbook

with Justin Schwartz

RUNNING PRESS

PHILADELPHIA · LONDON

Library of Congress Control Number: 2003096212

ISBN 0-7624-1833-8

Narrative Text Copyright © 2004 by Justin Schwartz
Recipes Copyright © 2004 by Durkee-Mower, Inc., except as follows:
Recipe page 99, Copyright © 2004 by Andy Schloss
Recipe page 100, Copyright © 2004 by Gale Gand
Recipe page 101, Copyright © 2004 by Carole Bloom
Recipe page 102, Copyright © 2004 by Sally Sampson
Recipe page 104, Copyright © 2004 by Carolyn Beth Weil
Recipe page 106, Copyright © 2004 by Dede Wilson
Recipe page 108, Copyright © 2004 by Dede Wilson
Recipe page 110, Copyright © 2004 by Lauren Chattman
Recipe page 111, Copyright © 2004 by Lora Brody
Recipe page 112, Copyright © 2004 by Tish Boyle
Recipe page 114, Copyright © 2004 by Dorie Greenspan
Recipe page 116, Copyright © 2004 by Nicole Kaplan
Recipe page 118, Copyright © 2004 by Bruce Weinstein and Mark Scarbrough
Recipe page 120, Copyright © 2004 by Lee Zalben
Recipe page 122, Copyright © 2004 by Duane Winfield
Recipe page 123, Copyright © 2004 by Jonathan King and Jim Stott
Recipe page 124, Copyright © 2004 by King Arthur Flour

Cover photography by Michael Weiss
Cover food styling by Maria Soriano
Cover and interior design by Corinda Cook
Typography: Avenir, Bodega Sans, and Monotype Sorts

This book may be ordered by mail from the publisher. Please include $2.50 for postage and handling.
But try your bookstore first!

Running Press Book Publishers
125 South Twenty-second Street
Philadelphia, Pennsylvania 19103-4399

Visit us on the web!
www.runningpress.com

Contents

The Story of Fluff

It was way back on May 14, 1920 when a small article appeared in the Lynn, Massachusetts *Daily Evening Item* announcing that two young men, H. Allen Durkee and Fred L. Mower, both graduates of Swampscott High and veterans of the United States field artillery in World War I, had formed a partnership in the manufacture of Marshmallow Fluff. The actual date they started working together remains a bit of a mystery, but it all started with the two of them cooking their confections in the kitchen at night and selling them door-to-door to housewives in the daytime.

As Durkee wrote in 1930: "Ten years ago we started out with one barrel of sugar (at 28 cents per pound), a few tin cans, two spoons, one second hand Ford, and no customers, but plenty of prospects. Today (after a short span of only ten years) we have through the fine cooperation of the wholesale grocers, the largest distribution of marshmallow creme in New England, and no Ford."

Were Durkee and Mower the creators of Marshmallow Fluff? Not quite. The recipe was tweaked over the years. For example, Fluff has gone from being made with dry sugar to liquid, because the liquid sugar is easier to work with. The origins of Fluff actually date back to 1917. Before World War I, a Somerville, Massachusetts, man named Archibald Query made Fluff in his candy factory and sold it. As was typical of the period, wartime shortages of staples like sugar forced him to close down. By the time the war was over, Query had other work and was not interested in restarting his business, but he was willing to sell the formula and the name "Marshmallow Fluff."

Durkee and Mower, back from the war and serving as reservists for the Yankee Division in the National Guard out of Topsfield, Massachusetts, pooled their savings and bought the recipe for five hundred dollars, not a small amount of money in those days. Having spent time in France during the war, they cleverly renamed their product Toot Sweet Marshmallow Fluff (a play on the French term "tout de suite"), but this turned out to be short-lived in favor of simply Marshmallow Fluff, as, of course, it's still known today.

What interested these two Massachusetts men in the business of producing and selling Marshmallow Fluff in the first place? Fred Mower had some experience working for a candy company in Boston. When he teamed up with Allen Durkee,

they originally tried to start their own company producing hard candies such as lollipops and ribbon candy. They worked out of a space that they rented from Durkee's father, George Durkee, no more than a mile away from the present day Durkee-Mower headquarters. It didn't take long for the pair to realize the candy business is a seasonal one with a relatively limited market. They turned to researching products for use in home kitchens. It's unclear how they first heard about Archibald Query's recipe for Marshmallow Fluff, which was no longer in production, but it piqued their interest. In no time, Durkee and Mower were producing Fluff themselves and taking their business door-to-door.

You might wonder what recommendations Durkee and Mower made to housewives for using Marshmallow Fluff in the kitchen. Fluff can labels dating all the way back to 1923 tell the story. Even in those early days, there were dozens of suggested uses for Fluff. Though it was quite a bit different from the now-famous Never-Fail Fudge recipe on jars today, there was a recipe for fudge on the back of the can, along with a list of sandwich ideas. No one had yet coined the name "Fluffernutter," but the first sandwich on the list was the clever combination of Fluff and peanut butter. Fluff, mayonnaise, pineapple, and almonds is a combination thankfully gone by the wayside. Other serving suggestions included using Fluff as a cream for hot chocolate and soda fountain delicacies; to flavor cake frostings; as a heated sauce for bread pudding or hot gingerbread; to make meringue for topping lemon pie; and to mix into fruit salads.

There was no shortage of creative ideas for using Marshmallow Fluff at home, and so the situation of "no customers, but plenty of prospects" didn't last long. An early receipt dating back to 1920 from the company's scrapbooks records a sale in April, 1920 of three one-gallon cans to a vacation lodge in New Hampshire. The price at the time? Just one dollar per gallon! Even now, Marshmallow Fluff remains one of the best values you can find in the supermarket. Selling their product door-to-door gained Durkee-Mower a fine reputation among local housewives and eventually placed Fluff on the shelves of local grocery stores. The business grew from there, and by 1927 Durkee-Mower were advertising Fluff prominently in Boston newspapers.

Fluff was so profitable that in 1929 Durkee-Mower moved the company to a factory on Brookline Street in East Lynn, more than tripling

their floor space to ten thousand square feet. The staff grew by four, bringing their numbers to ten. Next Durkee-Mower entered the hot chocolate business by merging with the Cream of Chocolate Company, makers of Rich's Instant Sweet Milk Cocoa. The name Rich's Instant Sweet Milk Cocoa didn't exactly roll off the tongue, so in 1937 they shortened the name Sweeco and made it more prominent on the label. A large newspaper advertising campaign followed, and the cocoa's sales increased rapidly. Durkee-Mower continued to make Sweeco until 1962.

The company was a pioneer in radio advertising when in 1930 they began sponsoring the weekly *Flufferettes* radio show on the Yankee Broadcasting Company radio network, which included twenty-one stations broadcasting to all of

New England. The fifteen-minute program, which aired on Sunday evenings just before *The Jack Benny Show*, included live music and comedy skits. *Flufferettes* served as a steppingstone to national recognition for a number of talented performers through the late 1940s.

Some of the earliest *Flufferettes* shows included the Book-of-the-Moment Dramas, a series of thirteen short comic sketches in which a fictional scholar with the proper Bostonian name of Lowell Cabot Boswell confronted some creatively rewritten moments in American history, from the Revolutionary War to the Harvard-Yale bicycle race. At the end of each episode, the narrator reported Boswell's departure to continue work on a mysterious book, assumed to be a historical text of monumental importance. The last episode revealed Boswell's

book as a collection of recipes for cakes, pies, candies, frostings, and other confections, all made with Marshmallow Fluff and appropriately entitled *The Yummy Book*. Updated several times over the years, the very best *Yummy Book* recipes are within these pages.

Even through the Great Depression, Durkee-Mower fared well enough to purchase a two-story factory in 1934. World War II brought shortages and rationing, not unlike the ones that halted production of Fluff during World War I under its original ownership. Existing sugar supplies were rationed to the corporations deemed more important. Unwilling to alter the recipes or reduce their quality standards for Fluff and Sweeco, Durkee-Mower was forced to cut production back considerably. In the interest of fairness, Fluff and

Sweeco were allotted to distributors on a percentage basis, quotas determined by pre-war sales records. During this period in American history, the company used its resources to promote the war effort in various ways: they converted part of the factory to wrap war-critical electronic and optical parts in special waterproof packaging. With little Fluff to sell, the *Flufferettes* show threw its advertising support behind the armed forces, particularly the Navy, because Allen Durkee's two older sons served during the war.

Meanwhile, Durkee-Mower planned for the future. They built a modern office building in 1945, adjacent to the factory purchased eleven years earlier. When industrial sugar rationing ended in 1947, the company prepared for expansion. First came a redesign of the Fluff packaging. New England housewives were polled. Customers thought Fluff should be in a jar short enough to store in the refrigerator—though Fluff requires no refrigeration. They also wanted the container made to fit a tablespoon for easy scooping. The company also added

a stippled surface to the jar, above and below the label, for a stronger and more easily gripped package. The same jar is still in use today, its longevity an unequaled testament to quality and reliability.

Once Durkee-Mower completed the jar redesign, they needed a factory efficient enough to produce Fluff. When the new operation opened in 1950, it was one of the most modern food manufacturing plants in the country. Much of the machinery was specially designed for Durkee-Mower. New filling and capping machines increased the speed of production from 80 to 125 jars per minute. Though much of the factory line was automated, their plans included increasing production, allowing them to automate without laying off any employees. But a clean and sanitary environment was more important than speed and efficiency. Wherever Marshmallow Fluff was exposed to air, the room was air conditioned or dehumidified or both. Sanitary tiles covered the walls and floors to facilitate a daily scouring, which even today takes the crew almost two hours to complete. The company takes every conceivable precaution to protect the purity of Marshmallow Fluff. They even switched from using granular sugar in hundred-pound bags to liquid sugar stored in 5500-gallon stainless steel tanks. This care and absence of preservatives makes it unnecessary to refrigerate Fluff.

Marshmallow Fluff's notoriety grew even more in 1956 when the company collaborated with Nestlé in a nationwide advertising campaign that won the Promotion of the Year Award. A new recipe for fudge appeared in *Ladies' Home Journal* and other notable magazines. This fudge was quick and easy to prepare and became so popular that the same recipe is still found on the back of every jar of Fluff today (see page 77). More recently, Durkee-Mower developed an easy-to-make cheesecake recipe, known as Lynne's Cheesecake (see page 45). It is also a family favorite, easily varied with different piecrusts, flavorings, and fruit toppings to suit personal tastes.

Marshmallow Fluff is prepared in much the same way now as it was in the 1950s. There are no new factories, but there is improved packaging and more efficient production, making this American favorite better and less expensive. For example, the company introduced an economy-sized 13-ounce jar in 1965. In 1966 a new high-ceiling warehouse was built to accommodate high stacking fork trucks. Palletized loading and unloading of trailers greatly reduced breakage and speeded up the shipping process. A pioneer in the use of plastic food containers, Durkee-Mower introduced the 1-pound-size jar in 1969. The new jar featured a wider mouth and straight-sided, slightly tapering walls for easier access and an airtight snap-on lid. Because the new jar can withstand temperature changes from freezing to boiling, it's even better for storing leftovers, and the lightweight and stackable jars help reduce warehousing and shipping costs.

Even today, Fluff is mixed one batch at a time in 13 Hobart mixers—sort of like giant KitchenAid stand mixers. Two members of the twenty-two person staff made up of engineers and electricians are devoted to maintaining these mixers, tuning them up, and replacing parts as necessary. More modern continuous methods for making generic marshmallow creme are available, but it's Durkee-Mower's special batch process that gives Fluff such a unique and fluffy texture. In this modern world, Durkee-Mower manages to preserve traditions. The company has remained an independent, family-owned business. When Fred Mower passed away, the Durkee family purchased his share of the company. Then Donald and Bruce Durkee, sons of co-founder Allen Durkee, joined the business. Bruce ran the company until he retired in 1982, when Donald took over as president. Donald's son Jonathan "Jon" Durkee joined the company in 1986 and will likely lead in years to come. Buyout offers from larger corporations are not uncommon, but are always refused. The downside to modernizing the production process is that it costs more to make Fluff according to such high standards. But Durkee-Mower believes the quality of their product is worth the added expense. Apparently customers agree because Fluff has been a family favorite for generations.

Despite the high cost of production, unit transportation costs have been reduced in recent years, allowing Durkee-Mower to sell Fluff for the best price possible. That's why you won't find Fluff on the West Coast. It's still just too costly to make Fluff in Lynn, Massachusetts, and ship it all the way across the country. You also won't often find very many advertisements for Fluff in newspapers and magazines. You won't find coupons either. And unlike many food companies, Durkee-Mower doesn't make premium items like t-shirts, baseball hats, sweatshirts, and banners. But they do sell a beach towel on their Web site at www.marshmallowfluff.com.

Business continues to expand. A new generation of youngsters enjoys Fluff the same way their parents and grandparents did before them. Fluff is now enjoyed in Canada, the United Kingdom, France, Germany, Holland, Israel, South Africa, Belgium, and the United Arab Emirates. Though Fluff enjoys wide distribution in the United States, there are still a few places where it's unavailable. If you happen to live in such a place, or cannot find Fluff locally, it may be ordered directly from the factory. Customers can purchase Fluff over the Web at www.marshmallowfluff.com.

Marshmallow Fluff Conversions

- One 7$\frac{1}{2}$-ounce jar Marshmallow Fluff measures approximately 2$\frac{1}{2}$ cups and equals 32 marshmallows . . . and there's no cutting or melting necessary!

- One 16-ounce plastic tub of Marshmallow Fluff measures approximately 5 cups and equals 5$\frac{1}{2}$ dozen marshmallows.

- One tablespoon of Marshmallow Fluff equals 1 marshmallow.

Super Sandwiches

fluffernutter

This longtime New England sandwich favorite is one of the most popular sandwiches in the country. It's quick, easy, and delicious. The "Fluffernutter" flavor combination also makes a delicious topping for puddings and cakes.

Serves 1

2 slices sandwich bread

Smooth peanut butter

Marshmallow Fluff

• Spread one slice of the bread with peanut butter. Top with a generous layer of Marshmallow Fluff. Top with the remaining slice of bread and cut. There you have it: a Fluffernutter!

What's the best type of bread for a Fluff sandwich?
According to Donald Durkee,
using whatever type of bread you happen
to have around will do just fine.
But he personally prefers toasted homemade bread.

Try these other delicious sandwich fillings too:

Cheese-Nut

Makes about $^2/_3$ cup

1/4 cup Marshmallow Fluff

3 ounces (6 tablespoons) cream cheese, softened

1/2 teaspoon prepared mustard

1 tablespoon chopped nuts

Dash of salt

2 slices Boston brown bread

• Mix together all of the ingredients and spread on the bread.

Orange-Peanut

Makes about $^1/_2$ cup

1/2 cup Marshmallow Fluff

1/4 cup crunchy peanut butter

1 tablespoon orange juice

1/2 teaspoon freshly grated orange zest

2 slices whole wheat bread

• Mix together all of the ingredients and spread on the bread.

Almond-Cream

Makes about ½ cup

½ cup Marshmallow Fluff

2 tablespoons butter or margarine, softened

2 to 3 tablespoons minced almonds, toasted

¼ teaspoon freshly grated lemon zest

2 slices date nut bread

• Mix together all of the ingredients and spread on the bread.

Tangy Prune

Makes about ½ cup

½ cup Marshmallow Fluff

¼ cup pureed prunes

1 teaspoon freshly squeezed lemon juice

⅛ teaspoon salt

2 slices bread, any kind

• Mix together all of the ingredients and spread on the bread.

Cherry-Cheese

Makes about 2/3 cup

1/4 cup Marshmallow Fluff

3 ounces (6 tablespoons) cream cheese, softened

2 tablespoons minced maraschino cherries

1/8 teaspoon salt

2 slices bread, any kind

• Mix together all of the ingredients and spread on the bread.

Cheese-Ginger

Makes about 2/3 cup

3 ounces (6 tablespoons) cream cheese, softened

Minced candied ginger, to taste

1/4 cup Marshmallow Fluff

2 slices bread, any kind

• Mix together the cream cheese and candied ginger. Add the Marshmallow Fluff and mix until blended. Spread on the bread.

Orange-Spice

Makes about ¹/₂ cup

¹/₂ cup Marshmallow Fluff

¹/₂ teaspoon freshly grated orange zest

¹/₈ teaspoon grated nutmeg

¹/₈ teaspoon salt

2 slices bread, any kind

• Mix together all of the ingredients and spread on the bread.

Cans of Fluff from the 1920s included other sandwich ideas such as:

* Marshmallow Fluff, dates, and cream cheese
* Marshmallow Fluff and jam or jelly
* Marshmallow Fluff and chopped nuts
* Marshmallow Fluff, mayonnaise, sliced apples, and walnuts
* Marshmallow Fluff, mayonnaise, bananas, and peanuts
* Marshmallow Fluff, mayonnaise, pineapple, and almonds

Cranberry-Orange

Makes about 1 cup

$1/2$ cup Marshmallow Fluff

$1/2$ cranberry-orange relish

2 slices any dark bread

• Mix together all of the ingredients and spread on the bread.

Apple Crisp Sandwich

Serves 1

$1/2$ cup Marshmallow Fluff

$1/2$ cup smooth peanut butter

$1/8$ teaspoon ground cinnamon

$1/2$ teaspoon freshly grated orange zest

2 slices sandwich bread

1 apple, sliced

• Mix together the Marshmallow Fluff, peanut butter, cinnamon, and orange zest. Spread on one slice of sandwich bread. Top with the apple slices and the remaining slice of bread.

Divine Salads and and Side Dishes

Frozen Fruit Salad

It's not a party without a cool, retro fruit salad. And a fruit salad made with Marshmallow Fluff is even better.

Serves 8

1 cup heavy whipping cream

1 cup Marshmallow Fluff

3 ounces (6 tablespoons) cream cheese, softened

$1/4$ cup mayonnaise

1 cup canned diced mixed fruit, drained

$1/2$ cup seedless red or green grapes

$1/2$ cup sliced strawberries

$1/2$ cup sliced bananas

$1/2$ cup drained and chopped canned pineapple

- In a mixing bowl, stir $1/4$ cup of the heavy cream into the Marshmallow Fluff. Stir in the cream cheese and mayonnaise.
- In a separate mixing bowl, whip the remaining $3/4$ cup heavy cream until it is stiff enough to form peaks. Fold the whipped cream into the Fluff mixture. Add the fruit and fold with a large spatula to combine. Pour into a 1-quart melon mold and freeze.

Molded Fruit Salad

Variations are listed below for inspiration, but just about any canned (or even frozen, thawed) fruit will work in this recipe. Pick your one or two favorites—pineapple, mandarin oranges, raspberries—and be creative.

Serves 6

One 3-ounce package fruit-flavored gelatin

2 cups hot water

$1/2$ cup Marshmallow Fluff

$1^1/2$ cups canned diced mixed fruit, drained

• In a mixing bowl, dissolve the gelatin in the hot water. Stir in the Marshmallow Fluff, mixing thoroughly. Chill the mixture until thickened and mounds form when dropped from a spoon. Fold in the fruit and pour into individual molds or custard cups. Chill until firm, up to 4 hours or overnight.

Variations:

Holiday Peach:

Prepare with lemon-flavored gelatin, $1^1/4$ cups drained diced canned peaches (in place of the mixed fruit), and $1/4$ cup chopped diced glacéed fruits (fruitcake mix).

Nut and Grape:

Prepare with lime-flavored gelatin, 1 cup seedless grapes (in place of the mixed fruit), and $1/2$ cup chopped walnuts.

Cherry-Almond:

Prepare with cherry-flavored gelatin, $1^1/4$ cups canned dark cherries, halved and pitted (in place of the mixed fruit), and $1/4$ cup toasted slivered almonds.

Apricot-Cherry:

Prepare with lemon-flavored gelatin, $1^1/4$ cups drained diced canned apricots (in place of the mixed fruit) and $1/4$ cup drained sliced maraschino cherries.

Pineapple-Orange Mallow Salad

Serves 6

2 cups drained canned pineapple chunks, reserving 2 tablespoons syrup

4 oranges, peeled and sectioned

2 cups Marshmallow Fluff

1 teaspoon freshly grated orange zest

• In a mixing bowl, toss the pineapple and orange sections together. In another bowl, combine the Marshmallow Fluff, reserved pineapple syrup, and orange zest and blend well. Spoon the fruit into a serving dish and top with the Fluff sauce.

Though sales of strawberry Fluff greatly outpace sales of the raspberry variety, the raspberry flavor was actually developed first. It was created in response to a request from a supermarket chain that felt there was ample demand for such a product.

fluffed Dressings

Fluff-Cheese Sauce

This and other Fluff dressings add a gourmet touch to fruits and molded salads.

Makes 1 cup

1 cup small curd cottage cheese

1/2 cup Marshmallow Fluff

2 teaspoons freshly squeezed lemon juice

1/4 teaspoon salt

• In a mixing bowl, combine the cottage cheese, Marshmallow Fluff, lemon juice, and salt. Mix thoroughly. Cover and chill until ready to use.

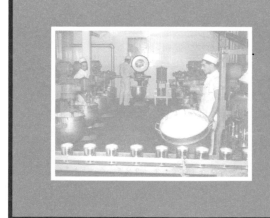

Marshmallow Fluff is still produced by the same batch-whipped process developed by Durkee-Mower more than 75 years ago, and it's the only marshmallow creme made in this manner. It's this special technique that makes Marshmallow Fluff so fluffy and gives it such great texture.

Fluff Cream

Makes 1³/₄ cups

1 cup sour cream

¹/₂ cup Marshmallow Fluff

¹/₄ teaspoon salt

¹/₈ teaspoon grated nutmeg

• In a mixing bowl, combine the sour cream, Marshmallow Fluff, salt, and nutmeg. Mix thoroughly, cover, and chill until ready to use.

Fluff-Lemon Mayonnaise

Makes 1¹/₂ cups

¹/₂ cup Marshmallow Fluff

1 tablespoon freshly squeezed lemon juice

¹/₂ teaspoon freshly grated lemon zest

1 cup mayonnaise

• In a mixing bowl, combine the Marshmallow Fluff and lemon juice. Mix in the lemon zest and the mayonnaise, ¹/₄ cup at a time, until smooth.

Durkee-Mower, the makers of Marshmallow Fluff, became a pioneer in radio advertising when in 1930 they began to sponsor the weekly *Flufferettes* radio show on the Yankee radio network, which included twenty-one stations broadcasting to all of New England. The fifteen-minute show, aired on Sunday evenings just before *The Jack Benny Show*, included live music and comedy skits, and served as a steppingstone to national recognition for a number of talented performers. The show continued through the late 1940s.

Special Side Dishes

Sweet Potato Soufflé

For something a bit different, try this delightful variation on traditional candied yams for your next holiday dinner.

Serves 6 to 8

Two 29-ounce cans sweet potatoes, drained

3 large eggs, beaten

$1/4$ cup milk, warmed

2 tablespoons butter or margarine, melted

$1/2$ teaspoon salt

One 7 $1/2$-ounce jar Marshmallow Fluff

• Preheat the oven to 425°F.

• Lightly grease a $2^{1}/_{2}$-quart soufflé dish or casserole and set aside.

• In a large mixing bowl, beat the sweet potatoes on medium speed until smooth. Beat in the eggs, milk, butter, salt, and one-third of the Marshmallow Fluff until combined. Pour the mixture into the prepared dish and bake for 20 minutes. Remove from the oven and increase the oven temperature to 550°F.

• Spread the remaining Fluff on top of the sweet potatoes, spreading to the edges. Return to the oven for 5 to 7 minutes more, or until the top is puffed and lightly browned.

Holiday Sweet Potatoes

Here's another spin on a holiday classic. To cook the sweet potatoes in a hurry, arrange them on a microwave-safe plate, cover with plastic wrap, and cook on high for 10 to 12 minutes (based on a 600-watt oven), or until tender.

Serves 6 to 8

4 large sweet potatoes, peeled, cooked, and cut into chunks, or one 40-ounce can sweet potatoes, drained

One 8-ounce can pineapple chunks, drained

¼ teaspoon ground cinnamon

One 7½-ounce jar Marshmallow Fluff

¼ cup (½ stick) butter or margarine

1 cup coarsely chopped walnuts

- Preheat the oven to 325°F.

- Arrange the sweet potatoes and pineapple in a shallow 2-quart baking pan and sprinkle with the cinnamon.

- In a small saucepan, combine the Marshmallow Fluff and butter and bring to a boil over high heat, stirring constantly. Pour over the sweet potato mixture and sprinkle with the walnuts. Bake for 15 to 20 minutes, until hot and bubbling.

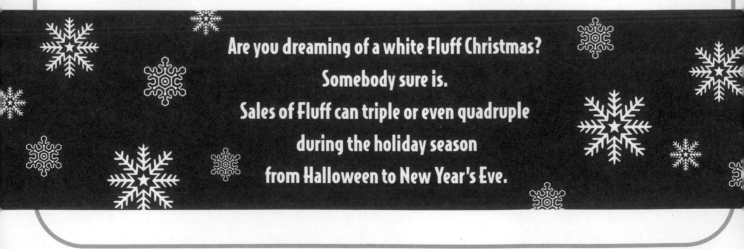

Are you dreaming of a white Fluff Christmas?
Somebody sure is.
Sales of Fluff can triple or even quadruple
during the holiday season
from Halloween to New Year's Eve.

Perfect Pies

Lemon Meringue Pie

Lemon pie with a fluff-flavored meringue topping—it's an extra-sweet variation on an American favorite.

Serves 8

1½ cups sugar

6 tablespoons cornstarch

¼ teaspoon salt

½ cup freshly squeezed lemon juice

½ cup cold water

3 large egg yolks, slightly beaten

1½ cups boiling water

1 tablespoon unsalted butter or margarine

One baked 9-inch piecrust

One recipe Fluff Meringue (recipe follows)

- In a medium saucepan, combine the sugar, cornstarch, and salt. Add the lemon juice, cold water, and egg yolks. Stir to combine, then stir in the boiling water. Cook over medium heat, stirring constantly, until the mixture begins to boil. Boil for 2 to 3 minutes. Stir in the butter until melted, and remove from the heat and let cool.

- While the filling is cooling, preheat the oven to 350°F and prepare the Fluff Meringue (see recipe below).

- Pour the cooled filling into the piecrust. Spread the meringue over the cooled filling, sealing well to form a top crust. Bake 10 to 12 minutes, or until the meringue is golden. Cool completely on a wire rack before serving.

Fluff Meringue

3 large egg whites, at room temperature

½ cup Marshmallow Fluff

- In a medium mixing bowl, beat the egg whites on medium-high speed until soft peaks form. Beat in the Marshmallow Fluff, a little at a time, until the whites stand in stiff glossy peaks. Use immediately.

Mocha-Meringue Ice Cream Pie

Serve this on a warm summer night for a refreshing treat.

Serves 8

3 large egg whites

$1/4$ teaspoon salt

$1/4$ teaspoon cream of tartar

$1/2$ teaspoon vanilla extract

One $7^1/2$-ounce jar Marshmallow Fluff

1 quart coffee ice cream, softened

Fluff-Fudge Sauce (see recipe page 88), for serving

• Preheat the oven to 300°F.

• In a large mixing bowl with a mixer on high speed, beat the egg whites until foamy. Add the salt, cream of tartar, and vanilla and continue beating until soft peaks form. Gradually beat in the Marshmallow Fluff and continue beating until very stiff peaks form. Spoon the mixture around the bottom and sides of a 9-inch pie plate. Bake 50 to 60 minutes. Turn off the heat and let the meringue shell sit in the closed oven for 1 hour. When completely cooled, spoon the ice cream into the shell. Place in the freezer until firm. Serve with Fluff-Fudge Sauce.

Rocky Road Pie

Inspired by the chunky ice cream flavor Rocky Road, this pie is not for the faint of heart.

Serves 8

1 quart chocolate ice cream, softened

$\frac{1}{2}$ cup chopped peanuts

$\frac{1}{4}$ cup semisweet chocolate chips, coarsely chopped

$\frac{1}{2}$ cup Marshmallow Fluff

$\frac{1}{4}$ cup chocolate syrup

One baked Graham Cracker Crust (recipe follows)

• In a large bowl, combine the ice cream with the peanuts and chopped chocolate. Spoon the Marshmallow Fluff and chocolate syrup into the ice cream mixture, swirling gently to create a marbled effect. Spoon into the piecrust and freeze until firm.

Graham Cracker Crust

Twenty-four 2-inch graham crackers, crushed

$\frac{1}{3}$ cup unsalted butter or margarine, melted

$\frac{1}{4}$ cup sugar

• Preheat the oven to 350°F.
• In a medium bowl, combine the cracker crumbs, butter, and sugar and mix until blended. Using the back of a spoon, press into the bottom and sides of a deep-dish 9- or 10-inch pie plate, or a 9-inch springform pan. Bake for 10 minutes and let cool before filling.

Yogurt Torte

Tangy lemon, nutty goodness, and Fluff, of course, combine for an altogether unique dessert.

Serves 10 to 12

One 6-ounce can walnuts, ground (1 1/2 cups)

1/4 cup sugar

1/4 cup (1/2 stick) unsalted butter or margarine, softened

Two 8-ounce packages cream cheese, softened

One 7 1/2-ounce jar Marshmallow Fluff

2 cups (16 ounces) lemon yogurt

- Preheat the oven to 350°F.
- Reserve 1/4 cup of the ground walnuts for garnish. Use a small bowl and a fork to mix together the remaining walnuts, sugar, and butter. Press the nut mixture firmly into the bottom of an 8- or 9-inch springform pan. Bake for 12 to 15 minutes, or until lightly golden. Remove from the oven and let cool before proceeding.
- In a large bowl, beat the cream cheese and Marshmallow Fluff until smooth. Stir in the lemon yogurt. Spread evenly over the cooled crust. Freeze until firm, about 2 1/2 hours.

Pumpkin Chiffon Pie

Try this recipe as a light and fluffy alternative to traditional pumpkin pie for your next Thanksgiving dinner.

Serves 6 to 8

One envelope unflavored gelatin

$1/2$ cup cold water

One 16-ounce can pumpkin puree

One $7^{1}/_{2}$-ounce jar Marshmallow Fluff

$1/2$ teaspoon ground ginger

$1/2$ teaspoon ground cinnamon

$1/4$ teaspoon grated nutmeg

$1/2$ teaspoon salt

$1/2$ cup heavy whipping cream

One baked Graham Cracker Crust (see recipe page 37)

- In a medium saucepan, combine the gelatin and cold water. Let stand 1 minute. Cook over low heat, stirring constantly, until the gelatin is completely dissolved, and remove from the heat. Stir in the pumpkin, Marshmallow Fluff, ginger, cinnamon, nutmeg, and salt. Refrigerate until the mixture mounds when dropped from a spoon.
- In a mixing bowl, beat the heavy cream on high speed until soft peaks form. Fold the whipped cream into the thickened gelatin mixture. Pour into the piecrust and refrigerate until set, about 2 hours.

Variations:

Strawberry, Raspberry, or Banana Chiffon Pie:

In place of the pumpkin and spices, substitute 2 cups mashed fruit, 1 tablespoon freshly squeezed lemon juice, and 1 teaspoon freshly grated lemon zest.

The Durkee-Mower factory in Lynn, Massachusetts, produces 30,000 pounds of Fluff per ten-hour day, four days a week.

Grasshopper Pie

They don't make mint-flavored Marshmallow Fluff, so try this recipe for St. Patrick's Day.

Serves 10

One envelope unflavored gelatin

$\frac{1}{2}$ cup cold water

One 7$\frac{1}{2}$-ounce jar Marshmallow Fluff

$\frac{1}{2}$ cup green crème de menthe liqueur

1$\frac{1}{2}$ cups heavy whipping cream

One Chocolate Crumb Crust (see recipe page 47)

- In a medium saucepan, combine the gelatin and cold water. Let stand 1 minute. Cook over low heat, stirring constantly, until the gelatin is completely dissolved. Remove from the heat. Stir in the Marshmallow Fluff and crème de menthe. Refrigerate until the mixture mounds when dropped from a spoon.

- In a mixing bowl, beat the heavy cream on high speed until soft peaks form. Fold the whipped cream into the thickened gelatin mixture. Pour into the piecrust and refrigerate until set, at least 4 hours or overnight.

fluffernutter Pie

The classic Fluffernutter flavor in pie form, with a chocolate crust, too.

Serves 6 to 8

One envelope unflavored gelatin

1 cup cold water

3 tablespoons sugar

1 teaspoon vanilla extract

1 cup Marshmallow Fluff

1 cup smooth peanut butter

2 cups heavy whipping cream

One Chocolate Crumb Crust (see recipe page 47)

- In a medium saucepan, combine the gelatin and ½ cup of the cold water. Let stand 1 minute. Cook over low heat, stirring constantly, until the gelatin is completely dissolved. Remove from the heat. Stir in the sugar, vanilla, and remaining ½ cup cold water. Beat in the Marshmallow Fluff and peanut butter. Refrigerate until the mixture mounds when dropped from a spoon.

- In a mixing bowl, beat the heavy cream on high speed until soft peaks form. Fold the whipped cream into the thickened gelatin mixture. Pour into the piecrust and refrigerate until set, at least 4 hours or overnight.

Fluff-Apple Pie

Another American favorite, made sweeter than ever with the addition of Fluff. Serve this pie to your family and don't tell them about the Fluff. They'll be pleasantly surprised when they take a bite.

Serves 6 to 8

5 to 6 cups peeled and sliced apples (2 to $2^1/_2$ pounds)

One unbaked 9-inch piecrust

1 cup Marshmallow Fluff

1 cup chopped raisins

2 tablespoons sugar

1 tablespoon freshly grated lemon zest

1 teaspoon freshly squeezed lemon juice

$^1/_2$ teaspoon salt

$^1/_8$ teaspoon ground cinnamon

For the Topping:

$^1/_2$ cup all-purpose flour

2 tablespoons unsalted butter or margarine

2 tablespoons light brown sugar

$^1/_2$ teaspoon ground cinnamon

- Preheat the oven to 375°F.

- Arrange the apple slices in the piecrust. In a mixing bowl, combine the Fluff with the raisins, sugar, lemon zest, lemon juice, salt, and cinnamon and blend thoroughly. Spread the mixture over the apples.

- To prepare the topping: In another bowl, combine the flour, butter, sugar, and cinnamon and mix together until crumbly. Sprinkle the topping over the pie. Bake for 35 to 40 minutes. Serve warm.

Meringue Shells

Fill these delicate, golden, and easy-to-prepare shells with sweetened fresh berries, diced fruit, creamy puddings, whipped cream, or sorbet (see pages 74 and 75).

Makes 6 shells

3 large egg whites, at room temperature

$1/2$ teaspoon cream of tartar

$1/4$ teaspoon salt

$1/4$ teaspoon vanilla extract

One 7 $1/2$-ounce jar Marshmallow Fluff

• Preheat the oven to 200°F.

• Line a large baking sheet with aluminum foil.

• In a large bowl with mixer on high speed, beat the egg whites until foamy. Add the cream of tartar and salt, then add the vanilla, and blend. Gradually beat in the Marshmallow Fluff. Continue beating until stiff peaks form. Spoon into six large mounds on the baking sheet. Use a teaspoon to shape the mounds into shells.

• Bake for 1 hour. Turn off the heat and let them sit in the oven for 1 hour longer. Carefully slide a spatula under each shell to loosen. Fill as desired.

Lynne's Cheesecake

This decades-old recipe is easy, reliable, and it tastes delicious, too.

Serves 12 to 14

Three 8-ounce packages cream cheese, softened

One 7½-ounce jar Marshmallow Fluff

3 tablespoons all-purpose flour

2 large eggs

One unbaked Graham Cracker Crust (see recipe page 37)

   or one 9-ounce ready-to-use crust

- Preheat the oven to 350°F.

- In a mixing bowl, mix together the cream cheese, Marshmallow Fluff, and flour until smooth. Add the eggs and mix just until blended. Pour into the crust. Bake for 45 minutes, or just until the edges begin to brown. Turn off the heat and let the cheesecake cool in the oven with the door slightly ajar for about 1 hour. Remove the cheesecake to a wire rack and cool completely. Cover and refrigerate for at least 4 hours before serving.

Variation:

Mocha Cheesecake:

Blend in 1 cup (6 ounces) semisweet chocolate chips, melted, and ¾ teaspoon instant coffee granules dissolved in ⅓ cup hot water when adding the Fluff.

Pumpkin Cheesecake

If you're looking for an out-of-the-ordinary dessert for Thanksgiving dinner, this is it.

Serves 12 to 14

Three 8-ounce packages cream cheese, softened

One 7$\frac{1}{2}$-ounce jar Marshmallow Fluff

4 large eggs

One 16-ounce can pumpkin puree

$\frac{1}{2}$ teaspoon ground ginger

$\frac{1}{2}$ teaspoon ground cinnamon

$\frac{1}{2}$ teaspoon grated nutmeg

$\frac{1}{4}$ teaspoon ground cloves

$\frac{1}{8}$ teaspoon salt

One unbaked Graham Cracker Crust (see recipe page 37) or one 9-inch ready-to-use crust

• Preheat the oven to 350°F.

• In a large mixing bowl with a mixer on medium speed, beat the cream cheese and Marshmallow Fluff until smooth. Add the eggs, pumpkin, ginger, cinnamon, nutmeg, cloves, and salt and mix just until blended. Pour into the crust and bake 45 minutes to 1 hour, or just until the edges begin to brown. Turn off the heat and let the cheesecake cool in the oven with the door slightly ajar for about 1 hour. Remove to a wire rack and cool completely. Cover and refrigerate for at least 4 hours before serving.

Chocolate Cheesecake

You will appease even diehard chocoholics with a chocolate cheesecake with chocolate crust.

Serves 12 to 14

2 cups (12 ounces) semisweet chocolate chips

Three 8-ounce packages cream cheese, softened

One 7½-ounce jar Marshmallow Fluff

1 cup sour cream

2 large eggs

One Chocolate Crumb Crust (recipe follows) or a 9-inch
   ready-to-use crust

• Preheat the oven to 375°F.

• In the top of a double boiler over simmering water, melt the chocolate, stirring frequently, and set aside.

• In a large mixing bowl with a mixer on medium speed, beat the cream cheese and Marshmallow Fluff until smooth. Add the sour cream and eggs and beat just until blended. Beat in the melted chocolate. Pour into the piecrust and bake for 45 minutes, or just until the edges begin to brown. Turn off the heat and let the cheesecake cool in the oven with the door slightly ajar for about 1 hour. Remove to a wire rack and cool completely. Cover and refrigerate for at least 4 hours before serving.

Note: You also can use a microwave oven set on high for 2 minutes to partially melt the chocolate, then stir until smooth and completely melted.

Chocolate Crumb Crust

20 Oreo cookies

6 tablespoons unsalted butter or margarine, melted

• Crush the cookies into fine crumbs and combine with the melted butter. Pour into an 8- or 9-inch springform pan and use the back of a spoon to press the crumb mixture into the bottom and up one inch on the sides of the pan. Alternatively, press the crumbs into a deep-dish 9- or 10-inch pie plate.

Fluff-Coffee Shake

Save yourself some money and skip that trip to the local coffee shop for overpriced gourmet coffee. You can whip up this in the blender at home in less than 1 minute.

Serves 1

1 cup cold milk

1 to 2 teaspoons instant coffee granules

2 tablespoons Marshmallow Fluff

• In a blender, combine the milk, instant coffee granules, and Marshmallow Fluff. Blend for 30 seconds or until smooth.

Frozen Hot Chocolate

This cocoa recipe will cool down the heat, even if it's the middle of July.

Serves 1

1 cup cold milk

2 tablespoons unsweetened cocoa

2 tablespoons Marshmallow Fluff

6 ice cubes

Grated chocolate, for garnish

• In a blender, combine the milk, cocoa, Marshmallow Fluff, and ice cubes. Blend for 30 seconds or until smooth. Garnish with grated chocolate.

Fluff-Fruit Shake

Just add your favorite fruit juice or, better yet, a combination of juices, to create this ice-cold, fruity, and refreshing smoothie.

Serves 1

1 cup cold fruit juice (orange, cranberry, grape, or apricot nectar)

2 tablespoons Marshmallow Fluff

3 ice cubes

• In a blender, combine the fruit juice, Marshmallow Fluff, and ice cubes. Blend for 30 seconds or until smooth.

Variation:
Super Fruit Fluff Shake:

• Add 1 small banana with the other ingredients.

Fluffernutter Shake

Add milk to your Fluffernutter sandwich recipe, but skip the bread! And you've got a sweet shake that will satisfy any peanut butter lover.

Serves 1

1 cup cold milk

2 tablespoons smooth peanut butter

2 tablespoons Marshmallow Fluff

• In a blender, combine the milk, peanut butter, and Marshmallow Fluff. Blend for 30 seconds or until smooth.

While New England consumes 65 percent of the world's Marshmallow Fluff, the appeal of the sweet stuff extends far beyond the United States. It's an international treat popular in England, France, Germany, Belgium, Dubai, and Israel, among other countries.

Dazzling Desserts, Cookies, and Bars

Fluff Corn Flake Kisses

These are delicate and delicious bits of crispy goodness.

Makes 12 kisses

1 large egg white

3 rounded tablespoons Marshmallow Fluff

$1/2$ teaspoon salt

$1/4$ cup sweetened flaked coconut

$1/4$ teaspoon almond extract

$1/4$ teaspoon vanilla extract

1 cup corn flakes

- Preheat the oven to 325°F.
- Grease a baking sheet. In a large mixing bowl, beat the egg white on medium-high speed until fluffy. Beat in the Marshmallow Fluff, salt, coconut, and almond and vanilla extracts. Gently stir in the corn flakes. Drop by spoonfuls onto the greased baking sheet. Bake for 20 to 25 minutes. Using a spatula, remove immediately to a rack to cool.

Variations:

Cherry-Almond:

Fold in $1/2$ cup toasted, slivered almonds with the corn flakes. Top each kiss with half a maraschino cherry and bake as directed.

Maple-Pecan:

Add $1/2$ teaspoon maple extract with the other extracts. Fold in $3/4$ cup chopped pecans with the corn flakes and bake as directed.

Date-Nut:

Add $3/4$ cup chopped walnuts and $3/4$ cup finely chopped, pitted dates along with the corn flakes and bake as directed.

Fluff Fudge Drops

Call them a cookie, call them a candy. Either way, they're sure to be a crowd pleaser.

Makes 4 dozen drop cookies

2 cups sugar

2 ounces unsweetened chocolate

1 cup milk

2 tablespoons unsalted butter or margarine

1 cup Marshmallow Fluff

2¼ cups graham cracker crumbs

½ cup chopped pecans

• In a medium saucepan, combine the sugar, chocolate, and milk. Cook over medium heat, stirring constantly, until the chocolate melts. Continue cooking and stirring until the mixture thickens, about 5 minutes. Remove from the heat and add the butter, but do not stir. Let the mixture cool until lukewarm.

• Stir in the Marshmallow Fluff, graham cracker crumbs, and pecans. Drop by spoonfuls onto waxed paper and let sit 2 hours to harden.

Help save the environment. Fluff's plastic 1-pound container can be reused for food storage and freezing.

Fluff Honey Bars

Makes 2 dozen bars

1 cup Marshmallow Fluff

1/3 cup unsalted butter or margarine

1/4 cup honey

1/4 cup sugar

1 large egg

1 teaspoon vanilla extract

1 cup all-purpose flour

1 teaspoon baking powder

1/2 teaspoon salt

3/4 cup chopped nuts

- Preheat the oven to 350°F.
- Grease a 9-inch square baking pan and set aside.
- In the top half of a double boiler over boiling water, combine the Marshmallow Fluff, butter, honey, and sugar. Cook, stirring, until thoroughly blended. Transfer the mixture to a bowl and let cool for 10 minutes. Beat in the egg and vanilla.
- In another bowl, sift together the flour, baking powder, and salt. Add it to the Fluff mixture with the chopped nuts and blend thoroughly. Turn the mixture into the greased baking pan. Bake for 25 minutes. Cool in the pan and cut into bars.

Walnut Bars

Makes 1 dozen bars

1 cup Marshmallow Fluff

$^1/_3$ cup unsalted butter or margarine

$^1/_2$ cup firmly packed dark brown sugar

1 large egg

1 teaspoon vanilla extract

1 cup all-purpose flour

1 teaspoon baking powder

$^1/_2$ teaspoon salt

1 cup chopped walnuts

- Preheat the oven to 350°F.

- Grease an 8-inch square baking pan and set aside.

- In the top of a double boiler over hot but not boiling water, combine the Marshmallow Fluff, butter, and brown sugar. Cook, stirring constantly, until thoroughly blended and smooth. Remove from the heat and allow to cool slightly. With a wooden spoon, beat in the egg and vanilla.

- In a mixing bowl, combine the flour, baking powder, and salt. Add the flour mixture to the Fluff mixture and stir just until blended. Fold in the walnuts. Spread in the prepared pan and bake 20 to 25 minutes, or until the bars begin to cook away from the sides of the pan. Cool completely before cutting.

Harvard Squares

Pack these bars in school lunches and you'll win some serious brownie points with your kids.

Makes 2 dozen bars

1/3 cup unsalted butter or margarine

1 1/2 cups graham cracker crumbs

One 7 1/2-ounce jar Marshmallow Fluff

1/3 cup milk

1 cup (6 ounces) semisweet chocolate chips

3 1/2 ounces sweetened flaked coconut

1 cup chopped walnuts

- Preheat the oven to 350°F.
- In a 13 x 9-inch baking pan, melt the butter over medium-low heat. Remove from the heat and sprinkle the graham cracker crumbs over the butter. Spread the mixture evenly over the bottom of the pan.
- In a small saucepan over low heat, combine the Marshmallow Fluff and milk, stirring until smooth. Pour over the crumbs. Top evenly with the chocolate chips, coconut, and walnuts and gently press down the mixture. Bake 25 to 30 minutes, or until lightly browned. Cool completely before cutting into 2-inch squares.

Marshmallow Fluff is made in strawberry and raspberry flavors, though the original accounts for 95 percent of sales. Why no chocolate Fluff? The butterfat in chocolate prevents Marshmallow Fluff from whipping properly.

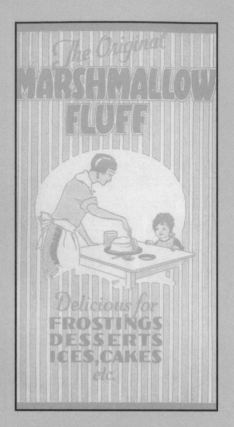

Fluff is gluten-free and kosher too!

Fluff Brownies

Makes 16 brownies

$1/2$ cup shortening

$1/2$ cup sugar

2 ounces semisweet chocolate, melted

2 large eggs

$1/2$ teaspoon vanilla extract

$1/2$ teaspoon salt

$1/2$ cup chopped walnuts

$2/3$ cup sifted all-purpose flour

$1/2$ teaspoon baking powder

$1/2$ cup Marshmallow Fluff

- Preheat the oven to 350°F.

- Grease an 8-inch square baking pan and set aside.

- In a mixing bowl, beat the shortening with the sugar until smooth. Stir in the melted chocolate. Add the eggs, vanilla, and salt and beat well. Add the nuts and stir.

- In another bowl, combine the flour and baking powder. Stir the flour into the chocolate mixture, just until blended. Add the Marshmallow Fluff and stir until blended. Spread the mixture into the prepared baking pan. Bake for 25 minutes. Cool completely and cut into squares.

Fluff Crispy Rice Treats

Crispy rice treats are delicious, but melting marshmallows is a tedious task. Using Marshmallow Fluff makes this favorite recipe so much easier to prepare.

Makes twenty-four 2-inch squares

1/4 cup (1/2 stick) unsalted butter or margarine

One 7 1/2-ounce jar Marshmallow Fluff

6 cups crispy rice cereal

- Grease a 13 x 9-inch baking pan and set aside.

- In a large saucepan over low heat, melt the butter. Add the Marshmallow Fluff and cook for about 5 minutes, stirring constantly. Remove from the heat. Add the crispy rice cereal and stir until well coated. Using a buttered spatula or waxed paper, press the mixture evenly into the baking pan. Cool completely, then cut into 2-inch squares.

Variations:

Strawberry or Raspberry Fluff Crispy Rice Treats:

Substitute one 7 1/2-ounce jar of either Strawberry Marshmallow Fluff or Raspberry Marshmallow Fluff for the regular Marshmallow Fluff in the recipe above.

Fluff Chocolate Crispy Rice Treats

Makes twenty-four 2-inch squares

$1/3$ cup unsalted butter or margarine

One $7^1/2$-ounce jar Marshmallow Fluff

2 cups (12 ounces) semisweet chocolate chips

5 cups crispy rice cereal

- Grease a 13 x 9-inch baking pan and set aside.

- In a large saucepan over low heat, melt the butter. Add the Marshmallow Fluff and cook for about 5 minutes, stirring constantly. Stir in the chocolate until melted and blended. Remove from the heat. Add the crispy rice cereal and stir until well coated. Using a buttered spatula or waxed paper, press the mixture evenly into the baking pan. Cool completely, then cut into 2-inch squares.

Sales of the 1-pound plastic tubs of Fluff account for about 60 percent of sales, while the famous $7^1/2$-ounce jars make up just about 40 percent.

Popcorn Fluff Puffs

Makes nine 3-inch puffs

One 7$\frac{1}{2}$-ounce jar Marshmallow Fluff

$\frac{1}{4}$ cup ($\frac{1}{2}$ stick) unsalted butter or margarine

8 cups popped unsalted, unbuttered popcorn (about $\frac{1}{4}$ cup
unpopped kernels)

- Grease a 9-inch square baking pan and set aside.

- In a microwave-safe dish, combine the Marshmallow
Fluff and butter. Cook on high in a microwave oven for 2
minutes (based on a 600-watt oven). Stir and cook 1
minute more. Or combine the Fluff and butter in a large
saucepan over medium-high heat and cook, stirring
constantly, until the mixture boils. Stir in the popcorn.
Using a buttered spatula or waxed paper, pat the mixture into the baking pan. Cool completely, then cut into
3-inch bars.

Whoopie Pies

Whether the Whoopie Pie originated from the Amish country in Pennsylvania or somewhere in Maine remains up for debate, but this Fluff version is a wonderful twist on the American classic.

Makes 15 pies

1 large egg

$1/3$ cup vegetable oil

1 cup sugar

2 cups all-purpose flour

$1/3$ cup unsweetened cocoa

1 teaspoon baking soda

$1/4$ teaspoon salt

$3/4$ cup milk

1 teaspoon vanilla extract

Filling (recipe follows)

- Preheat the oven to 350°F.

- Grease 2 large baking sheets and set aside.

- In a large bowl with a mixer on medium speed, beat the egg and vegetable oil until combined. Gradually beat in the sugar and continue beating until pale yellow in color.

- In another bowl, combine the flour, cocoa, baking soda, and salt. In a measuring cup, combine the milk and vanilla. Add the flour and milk mixtures alternately to the egg and sugar, beginning and ending with dry ingredients. Drop by tablespoons onto the baking sheets. These will spread a lot, so make 6 cakes per sheet at a time.

- Bake for about 5 minutes, or until the top springs back when lightly touched with a finger. Remove to wire racks to cool completely. When cool, sandwich the filling between two cakes to form the Whoopie Pies.

filling

¹/₂ **cup (1 stick) unsalted butter or margarine, softened**

1 cup confectioners' sugar

1 cup Marshmallow Fluff

1 teaspoon vanilla extract

• In a medium bowl with a mixer on medium speed, beat the butter with the sugar, Marshmallow Fluff, and vanilla until light and fluffy.

Special 5-pound tubs of Marshmallow Fluff are sold in price clubs and to some corporate customers. Unlike the jars, which are automatically filled by machine, every 5-pound tub is filled manually.

Chocolate Fluffernutter Bars

Even with the addition of healthy toasted-oat cereal, this recipe is far too rich and sweet to qualify as breakfast food.
Try serving these at the next bake sale.

Makes 12 bars

One 7½-ounce jar Marshmallow Fluff

2 tablespoons unsalted butter or margarine

½ cup smooth peanut butter

3 cups toasted-oat cereal (such as Cheerios)

1 cup chopped roasted peanuts

2 cups (12 ounces) semisweet chocolate chips

- Grease a 9-inch square baking pan and set aside.

- Place the Marshmallow Fluff and butter in a microwave-safe bowl. Cook on high in a microwave oven for
  1 minute (based on a 600-watt oven). Stir and cook for 1 minute more. Stir in the peanut butter and cook for
  1 minute more. Or combine the Fluff and butter in a medium saucepan over medium-high heat and cook,
  stirring constantly, until the mixture boils. Stir in the peanut butter and cook 1 minute more.

- In another large bowl, combine the cereal, peanuts, and half of the chocolate chips. Fold in the peanut
  butter–Fluff mixture to coat. Pour into the baking pan. Cover with waxed paper or plastic wrap and press firmly
  into the pan. Melt the remaining chocolate morsels in a microwave-safe bowl in the microwave oven or in the
  top of a double boiler over simmering water and spread on top of the bars. Set aside to cool completely
  before cutting into 12 bars.

Fluff Bread Pudding

Serves 4

2 cups milk

1 cup dry unseasoned breadcrumbs

¼ teaspoon salt

½ teaspoon almond extract

½ teaspoon vanilla extract

2 tablespoons unsalted butter or margarine, melted

2 large eggs, separated

½ cup Marshmallow Fluff

- Preheat the oven to 350°F.
- Grease a 1-quart baking pan and set aside.
- In a saucepan over medium heat, heat the milk, stirring regularly, just until it starts to simmer. In a large bowl, combine the breadcrumbs, salt, almond and vanilla extracts, melted butter, and the hot milk.
- In another bowl, combine the egg yolks and Marshmallow Fluff and beat well. In another bowl with a clean whisk or beaters, beat the egg whites until stiff and fold into the Fluff mixture. Add to the milk mixture and combine thoroughly. Turn into the prepared baking pan. Set the pan in a larger pan of hot water and bake for 1 hour.

Variation:

Queen Pudding:

Spread the top of the Fluff Bread Pudding with tart jelly. Cover with Fluff Meringue (see recipe page 35) and bake until the meringue is set, about 10 minutes more.

Chilly Treats

Lemon Fluff Soufflé

Serves 4 to 6

1½ cups milk

½ cup fine, dry unseasoned breadcrumbs

¼ cup (½ stick) unsalted butter or margarine, softened

¼ cup sugar

2 tablespoons freshly squeezed lemon juice

2 teaspoons freshly grated lemon zest

2 large eggs, separated

¼ teaspoon salt

½ cup Marshmallow Fluff

- Preheat the oven to 350°F.

- Lightly grease a 1-quart casserole or soufflé dish and set aside.

- In a medium bowl, combine the milk and breadcrumbs. Let stand to soften the crumbs. In a large bowl, cream the butter, sugar, lemon juice, and zest until smooth. Beat in the egg yolks and blend in the breadcrumb mixture.

- In another bowl with a clean whisk or beaters, beat the egg whites with the salt until stiff peaks form. Gently fold the egg-white mixture into the breadcrumb mixture and mix in the Marshmallow Fluff just until incorporated. Turn into the casserole. Place the dish in a larger pan of hot water and bake for 45 minutes.

If you're worried about keeping an opened jar of Fluff fresh and decide to store it in the refrigerator, be sure to let it warm up at room temperature before you try using it. It can take up to a full day for Fluff to return to its original, spreadable consistency.

Chocolate Mousse

Unlike most recipes for chocolate mousse, this one contains no raw eggs. So if you gave up on making mousse for fear of contaminated eggs, this recipe (and the vanilla version that follows) should come as a very welcome surprise.

Makes 1 ½ pints

1 ounce semisweet chocolate

1 cup Marshmallow Fluff

1 cup heavy whipping cream

½ teaspoon vanilla extract

- In the top of a double boiler over simmering water, melt the chocolate and combine with the Marshmallow Fluff in a mixing bowl. Stir in ¼ cup of the heavy cream and the vanilla. In another bowl with a mixer on high speed, beat the remaining ¾ cup of cream until thick but not stiff. Fold into the Fluff mixture. Freeze until firm, without stirring, and serve.

Vanilla Mousse

If you're feeling creative, there are all kinds of recipes in this book that can be made by substituting raspberry or strawberry Marshmallow Fluff, and this is one of them. Or you can try the fresh fruit variations listed below.

Makes 1¼ pints

One 7½-ounce jar Marshmallow Fluff

1 cup heavy whipping cream

1 teaspoon vanilla extract

• In a mixing bowl, combine the Marshmallow Fluff, ¼ cup of the whipping cream, and the vanilla. In another bowl with a mixer on high speed, beat the remaining ¾ cup of cream until thick but not stiff. Fold into the Fluff mixture. Freeze until firm, without stirring, and serve.

Variations:
Strawberry or Raspberry Mousse:

Prepare the Vanilla Mousse as directed and freeze until mushy. Add ¾ cup crushed and well-drained frozen strawberries or raspberries. Return to the freezer and freeze as directed above.

Apricot Freeze

Makes 1¹/₄ pints

2 cups canned apricots with canning syrup

¹/₄ teaspoon freshly grated lemon zest

1 tablespoon freshly squeezed lemon juice

1 cup Marshmallow Fluff

• Mash the apricots, with the canning syrup, through a sieve into a mixing bowl. In another bowl, combine the lemon zest and juice and Marshmallow Fluff. Add the mashed apricots a little at a time, mixing well after each addition. Freeze until firm, without stirring, and serve.

Variations:
Fruit and Berry Freezes:

Two cups of any canned fruit or berry will make a fine Freeze. Follow the directions for Apricot Freeze, replacing the apricots with any other fruit or berry. Purple Plum Freeze made with a teaspoon of mint extract is just as delicious as a side for roast lamb or a refreshing dessert.

Old-Fashioned Vanilla Ice Cream

For almost as long as Fluff has been in existence, cooks used it to make homemade ice cream. There's no cooking involved, so ask your kids to help the next time you make a batch.

Makes 1½ pints

1 cup milk

2 teaspoons vanilla extract

1¼ cup Marshmallow Fluff

1 cup heavy whipping cream

- In a mixing bowl, very slowly stir ¼ cup of the milk and the vanilla into the Marshmallow Fluff until smooth. Add the remaining ¾ cup milk and mix until smooth. In another mixing bowl with a mixer on high speed, beat the heavy cream until thick but not stiff. Fold into the Fluff mixture. Freeze to a mush. Beat the mixture until smooth. Return to the freezer and freeze until firm, without stirring, and serve.

Variations:

Banana Ice Cream:

Follow the Vanilla Ice Cream recipe until it has frozen to a mush and been beaten, then add 1 cup of mashed bananas and 2 teaspoons of freshly squeezed lemon juice and continue freezing. Makes about 1¾ pints.

Strawberry or Raspberry Ice Cream:

Follow the Vanilla Ice Cream recipe until it has frozen to a mush and been beaten, then add 1 cup of mashed berries and continue freezing. Makes about 1¾ pints.

Chocolate Ice Cream:

Follow the Vanilla Ice Cream recipe, stirring 2 ounces of melted semisweet chocolate into the Marshmallow Fluff before adding the milk and vanilla. Makes 1½ pints.

Southern Pecan Ice Cream

Makes 1½ pints

⅔ cup firmly packed dark brown sugar

⅓ cup water

⅔ cup Marshmallow Fluff

1 tablespoon unsalted butter or margarine

1½ cups pecan halves

1 cup heavy whipping cream

- In a medium saucepan, combine the sugar and water. Cook over medium-high heat, stirring constantly, until it reaches a temperature of 235°F on a candy thermometer (also known as the soft-ball stage—when a small amount of mixture dropped into very cold water forms a ball that flattens on removal from the water). Remove the saucepan from the heat and add the Marshmallow Fluff and butter, mixing well. Let cool completely. Add the pecans and stir.

- In a mixing bowl with a mixer on high speed, beat the cream until thick but not stiff. Fold the whipped cream into the Fluff mixture. Freeze to a mush. Beat the mixture until smooth. Return to the freezer and freeze until firm, without stirring, and serve.

Marshmallow Fluff sure is sticky. The easiest way to measure Fluff when making a recipe is to weigh the full container, then remove the desired measured amount by weight. Remember, a cup of Fluff weighs slightly more than 3 ounces. A 7½-ounce jar contains about 2½ cups, and a 16-ounce container contains about 5 cups. Most recipes do not require precise measurements of Marshmallow Fluff to be successful.

Angel Fluff

A dessert that's heavenly indeed.

Serves 5 to 6

$1/2$ cup heavy whipping cream

1 cup Marshmallow Fluff

$1^1/2$ cups drained, crushed canned pineapple

$1/3$ cup drained and halved maraschino cherries

2 ripe bananas, diced

3 cups angel food cake cubes or pieces

• In a mixing bowl with a mixer on high speed, beat the heavy cream until it's stiff enough to form peaks. Add the Marshmallow Fluff and mix thoroughly. Add the pineapple, maraschino cherries, bananas, and cake and fold in gently. Spoon into dessert glasses and chill for 1 to 2 hours before serving.

Rice and Pineapple Fluff

Serves 6

$1/2$ cup evaporated milk

1 tablespoon freshly squeezed lemon juice

1 cup Marshmallow Fluff

2 cups cold cooked white rice

1 cup drained, crushed canned pineapple, chilled

1 teaspoon vanilla extract

• Freeze the evaporated milk in ice cube trays until crystallized around the edges. Empty the cubes into a chilled mixing bowl and beat on high speed until very stiff, gradually adding the lemon juice. Fold in the Marshmallow Fluff, rice, pineapple, and vanilla. Spoon into chilled dessert dishes and serve at once.

There is no expiration date on jars of Fluff, but Fluff is best when used within six to twelve months from the date of purchase, depending upon the storage temperature. Cooler temperatures mean a longer shelf life.

Fluffy Strawberry Sorbet

An icy cold and far-from-sinful dessert. Try substituting raspberry or strawberry Marshmallow Fluff in this or any of the fruit sorbet recipes that follow.

Makes 1½ cups

One 16-ounce bag frozen unsweetened strawberries, partially thawed

½ cup water

1 teaspoon freshly squeezed lemon juice

One 7½-ounce jar Marshmallow Fluff

- In a blender or food processor, combine the strawberries, water, and lemon juice. Process until the berries are almost smooth, but some chunks of fruit remain. Add the Marshmallow Fluff and process until blended. Pour into an ice cream machine and freeze according to the manufacturer's instructions. As an alternative, pour into a shallow bowl and freeze for 3 or 4 hours, until slushy. Beat with an electric mixer or in a food processor to break up the ice crystals. Return to the freezer and freeze until firm.

fluffy Blackberry Sorbet

Makes 1¹/₂ cups

One 16-ounce can blackberries

¹/₂ cup water

1 teaspoon freshly squeezed lemon juice

One 7¹/₂-ounce jar Marshmallow Fluff

• Drain the blackberries, reserving ¹/₂ cup of liquid. In a blender or food processor, combine the blackberries, reserved liquid, and lemon juice. Process until the berries are almost smooth, but some chunks of fruit remain. Add the Marshmallow Fluff and process until blended. Pour into an ice cream machine and freeze according to the manufacturer's instructions. As an alternative, pour into a shallow bowl and freeze for 3 or 4 hours, until slushy. Beat with an electric mixer or in a food processor to break up the ice crystals. Return to the freezer and freeze until firm.

fluffy Peach Sorbet

Makes 1¹/₂ cups

One 29-ounce can peaches in juice, drained

1 teaspoon freshly squeezed lemon juice

One 7¹/₂-ounce jar Marshmallow Fluff

• In a blender or food processor, combine the peaches and lemon juice. Process until the berries are almost smooth, but some chunks of fruit remain. Add the Marshmallow Fluff and process until blended. Pour into an ice cream machine and freeze according to the manufacturer's instructions. As an alternative, pour into a shallow bowl and freeze for 3 or 4 hours, until slushy. Beat with an electric mixer or in a food processor to break up the ice crystals. Return to the freezer and freeze until firm.

Never-Fail Fudge

This is the classic back-of-the-jar recipe for which Marshmallow Fluff is perhaps best known. It's fun to eat and makes a thoughtful gift for friends and family.

Makes 2½ pounds

One 7½-ounce jar Marshmallow Fluff

2½ cups sugar

One 5.33-ounce can (¾ cup) evaporated milk

¼ cup (½ stick) unsalted butter or margarine

¾ teaspoon salt

2 cups (12 ounces) semisweet chocolate chips

¾ teaspoon vanilla extract

½ cup chopped walnuts (optional)

• Grease a 9-inch square baking pan and set aside.

• In a large, heavy saucepan, combine the Marshmallow Fluff, sugar, evaporated milk, butter, and salt. Cook, stirring, over low heat until blended, then increase the heat to high and bring to a full, rolling boil. Reduce the heat to medium-high and cook at a low boil, stirring constantly, for 5 minutes. Remove from the heat, add the chocolate and vanilla, and stir until the chocolate is melted and blended. Stir in the nuts, if using, and pour into the greased pan. Let cool until set and cut into small squares for serving.

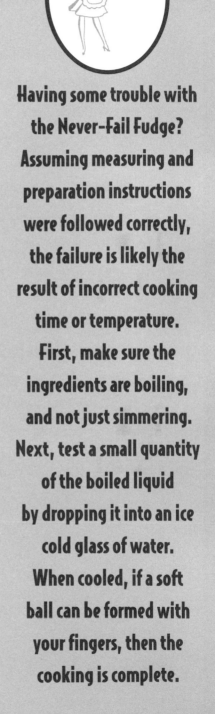

Having some trouble with the Never-Fail Fudge? Assuming measuring and preparation instructions were followed correctly, the failure is likely the result of incorrect cooking time or temperature. First, make sure the ingredients are boiling, and not just simmering. Next, test a small quantity of the boiled liquid by dropping it into an ice cold glass of water. When cooled, if a soft ball can be formed with your fingers, then the cooking is complete.

Microwave Fudge

Makes 2½ pounds

One 7½-ounce jar Marshmallow Fluff

2½ cups sugar

One 5.33-ounce can (¾ cup) evaporated milk

¼ cup (½ stick) unsalted butter or margarine

¾ teaspoon salt

2 cups (12 ounces) semisweet chocolate chips

¾ teaspoon vanilla extract

½ cup chopped walnuts, optional

- Grease a 9-inch square baking pan and set aside.

- In a microwave-safe bowl, combine the Marshmallow Fluff, sugar, evaporated milk, butter, and salt. Microwave, uncovered, on medium-high or 2½ minutes (based on a 600-watt oven). Remove from the oven and stir until blended. Set microwave on medium-high for 5 minutes more. Remove and stir until blended. Repeat microwaving on medium-high for 5 minutes. Remove and stir. Again, microwave on medium-high for 2½ minutes. Remove and stir again. Finally, microwave one last time on medium-high for 6 minutes more. Stir in the chocolate and vanilla and then the nuts until blended. Pour into the greased pan. Let cool until set and cut into small squares for serving.

Nutty Butterscotch Fudge

Makes 2½ pounds

One 7½-ounce jar Marshmallow Fluff

1 cup sugar

One 5.33-ounce can (¾ cup) evaporated milk

2 tablespoons unsalted butter or margarine

¾ teaspoon salt

One 12-ounce package butterscotch-flavored pieces

¾ teaspoon vanilla extract

½ cup salted peanuts, chopped

• Grease a 9-inch square baking pan and set aside.

• In a large, heavy saucepan, combine the Marshmallow Fluff, sugar, evaporated milk, butter, and salt. Bring to a full, rolling boil over medium heat and cook, stirring constantly, for 5 minutes. Remove from the heat and quickly stir in butterscotch pieces and vanilla until the pieces are melted. Stir in the peanuts and pour into the greased pan. Let cool until set and cut into small squares for serving.

Peanut Butter Fudge

There's just no end to the ways you can combine the flavors of peanut butter and Marshmallow Fluff!

Makes 1½ pounds

2 cups sugar

⅔ cup milk

One 7½-ounce jar Marshmallow Fluff

1 cup smooth or crunchy peanut butter

1 teaspoon vanilla extract

• Grease an 8-inch square baking pan and set aside.

• In a large, heavy saucepan, combine the sugar and milk. Cook over medium-high heat, stirring constantly, until it reaches a temperature of 235°F on a candy thermometer (also known as the soft-ball stage—when a small amount of mixture dropped into very cold water forms a ball that flattens on removal from the water). Remove from the heat, let cool slightly, and blend in the Marshmallow Fluff, peanut butter, and vanilla. Pour into the greased pan. Let cool until set and cut into small squares for serving.

Penuche

Makes 1³/₄ pounds

3 cups firmly packed brown sugar

1 cup light cream

1 tablespoon light corn syrup

2 tablespoons unsalted butter or margarine

1 cup Marshmallow Fluff

¹/₂ teaspoon vanilla extract

- Grease an 8-inch square baking pan and set aside.
- In a large saucepan over medium heat, combine the sugar, cream, and corn syrup. Heat to a full boil, stirring constantly. Cover and cook over medium heat for 3 minutes. Uncover and cook until it reaches a temperature of 235°F on a candy thermometer (also known as the soft-ball stage—when a small amount of mixture dropped into very cold water forms a ball that flattens on removal from the water). Add the butter and cool, without stirring, until lukewarm (110°F), about 45 minutes. The bottom of the pan will feel comfortably warm. Add the Marshmallow Fluff and vanilla, and beat with a wooden spoon until the mixture is thickened and begins to lose some of its gloss. Pour into the greased pan. Let cool until set and cut into small squares for serving.

Marshmallow Fluff expands and contracts with temperature changes. After rapid temperature changes, it requires sufficient time before the internal pressure is neutralized. Cupping and doming of the plastic lid occurs in the meantime.

Cocoa-Fluff Truffles

Make some truffles and fudge and give gift boxes to your friends.

Makes 1 pound

2²/₃ cups (16 ounces) semisweet chocolate chips

One 7¹/₂-ounce jar Marshmallow Fluff

Flavorings (see below)

• In the top of a double boiler over hot but not boiling water, heat the chocolate, stirring occasionally, until melted. Blend in the Marshmallow Fluff. Add your choice of flavorings (see below). Let cool slightly and shape into ¹/₂-inch balls.

Flavorings:

Peppermint:

Knead in 2 teaspoons peppermint extract. Roll the finished balls in chocolate sprinkles.

Coconut:

Roll the finished balls in sweetened flaked coconut.

Walnut:

Roll the finished balls in minced walnuts.

Cocoa-Fluff Chewies

Makes 2½ dozen

¼ cup unsweetened cocoa

2 tablespoons water

¼ cup smooth peanut butter

2 tablespoons Marshmallow Fluff

¾ cup bran flake cereal

½ cup seedless raisins

1 cup sweetened flaked coconut

• In a large bowl, blend the cocoa with the water until smooth. Add the peanut butter and Marshmallow Fluff and stir until thoroughly blended. Add the bran cereal, raisins, and ½ cup of the coconut. Form into 1-inch balls and roll in the remaining coconut to coat. These taste best if left to stand for an hour before serving.

Marshmallow Fluff is one of the best values in the supermarket. If you take inflation into account, Fluff is actually cheaper today than it was back in the 1940s and 1950s.

Apricot Fingers

Makes about 24 fingers

One 6-ounce package dried apricots

½ batch Fluff Fondant (see recipe below)

• Flatten each apricot half slightly. Level 1 teaspoon of Fluff Fondant, shape into a small oval, and use to stuff the apricots.

Fluff Fondant

Makes 3½ cups

One 7½-ounce jar Marshmallow Fluff

¼ teaspoon vanilla extract

About 2 cups confectioners' sugar

• In a small bowl, combine the Marshmallow Fluff and vanilla. Gradually stir in enough confectioners' sugar until the mixture is stiff enough to knead. Knead until the mixture loses its stickiness, adding more confectioners' sugar if necessary. Transfer the fondant to a bowl or jar and place a damp cloth over the top, then cover tightly. Store fondant in a cool place for 2 to 3 days before using.

Super Sauces

Butterscotch Sauce

Turn an ordinary bowl of ice cream into something special with a dollop of homemade hot Butterscotch Sauce.

Makes about 1 cup

$1/2$ cup Marshmallow Fluff

2 tablespoons unsalted butter or margarine

1 cup firmly packed light brown sugar

$1/2$ cup water

- Place the Marshmallow Fluff and butter in a mixing bowl and set aside.

- In a small saucepan, combine the sugar and water and cook over medium-high heat until it reaches a temperature of 235°F on a candy thermometer (also known as the soft-ball stage—when a small amount of mixture dropped into very cold water forms a ball that flattens on removal from the water), 4 to 5 minutes. Add the sugar mixture to the bowl with the Fluff and stir to combine. Serve hot or cold.

Chocolate-Peanut Sauce

Makes 3 cups

1 cup Marshmallow Fluff

1 cup chocolate syrup

1/2 cup smooth peanut butter

2/3 cup sour cream

1 teaspoon vanilla extract

- In the top of a double boiler over simmering water, combine the Marshmallow Fluff, chocolate syrup, peanut butter, and sour cream. Cook, stirring, until very smooth and thickened. Blend in the vanilla and serve hot.

Fluff Hard Sauce

This sauce is great served over hot plum pudding.

Makes about 2 cups

One 7 1/2-ounce jar Marshmallow Fluff

1/4 cup (1/2 stick) unsalted butter or margarine, softened

1 1/2 cups confectioners' sugar

1 tablespoon brandy

- In a small bowl with a mixer on medium speed, beat the Marshmallow Fluff with the butter and confectioners' sugar until smooth. Mix in the brandy.

Fluff-Rum Sauce

Makes 2 cups

¹/₂ cup heavy whipping cream

1 large egg white, at room temperature

¹/₄ teaspoon salt

1 cup Marshmallow Fluff

1 teaspoon rum extract

- In a mixing bowl with a mixer on high speed, beat the heavy cream until it's stiff enough to form peaks. Set aside. In a small bowl with a mixer on high speed, beat the egg white and salt until foamy. Gradually beat in the Marshmallow Fluff and rum extract. Continue beating until stiff peaks form. Fold in the whipped cream.

Have you ever spilled a little Fluff on your clothing or a tablecloth? Removing it is simpler than you'd think. If water will not damage the soiled material, warm water will dissolve Fluff quite easily.

Fluff-Fudge Sauce

With whipped cream and ice cream, you've got all the makings of a perfect sundae. Chopped walnuts and a maraschino cherry are optional.

Makes 2 cups

1 cup unsweetened cocoa

One 5.33-ounce can ($3/4$ cup) evaporated milk

One $7^1/2$-ounce jar Marshmallow Fluff

$1/2$ cup sugar

$1/3$ cup unsalted butter or margarine

$1/2$ teaspoon vanilla extract

• In a medium saucepan over medium-low heat, combine the cocoa and evaporated milk until well blended. Add the Marshmallow Fluff, sugar, and butter. Cook, stirring constantly, until the mixture is smooth and comes to a boil. Remove from the heat and stir in the vanilla. Serve warm.

Fluff-Chocolate Sauce

Makes 1$1/2$ cups

$1/4$ cup light cream

$1/4$ cup water

1 cup (6 ounces) semisweet chocolate chips

$1/2$ cup Marshmallow Fluff

• In a small saucepan over medium heat, combine the cream and water, stirring constantly, until the mixture comes to a boil. Remove from the heat and stir in the chocolate pieces until melted. Add the Marshmallow Fluff and blend until smooth and thick. Serve hot or cold.

Fluff-Cream Cheese Sauce

Makes about 2 cups

One 7 ½-ounce jar Marshmallow Fluff

One 8-ounce package cream cheese, softened

3 tablespoons orange juice

1 teaspoon freshly grated orange zest

• In a small bowl, combine the Marshmallow Fluff, cream cheese, orange juice, and orange zest until smooth.

Fluff-Banana Sauce

Fluff and bananas is a flavor combination made in Heaven. You may want to eat this straight from the bowl.

Makes about 1¼ cups

1 cup Marshmallow Fluff

1 ripe banana, mashed

1 teaspoon freshly squeezed lemon juice

½ teaspoon vanilla extract

¼ teaspoon freshly grated lemon zest

• In a mixing bowl, combine the Marshmallow Fluff, banana, lemon juice, vanilla, and lemon zest. Mix until smooth.

fabulous
frostings

Fluffernutter Frosting

This is the taste of a Fluffernutter sandwich in a frosting.

Makes enough to fill and frost two 8- or 9-inch cake layers

1 cup Marshmallow Fluff

1/2 cup smooth peanut butter

1/3 cup unsalted butter or margarine, softened

1 1/3 cups confectioners' sugar

1/4 teaspoon salt

2 tablespoons milk

1/4 teaspoon vanilla extract

• In a medium mixing bowl, beat the Marshmallow Fluff, peanut butter, and butter at low speed until blended. Increase the speed to medium and add the sugar and salt alternately with the milk, adding just enough milk to make the frosting smooth and spreadable. Beat in the vanilla.

Fluff Seven-Minute Frosting

This elegant frosting heaps high, fluffy, and glossy.

Makes enough to fill and frost two 8- or 9-inch cake layers

1 cup Marshmallow Fluff

2 egg whites, at room temperature

1/4 cup water

1 cup sugar

1/4 teaspoon cream of tartar

1/8 teaspoon salt

1 teaspoon vanilla extract

• In the top of a double boiler over hot but not boiling water, combine the Marshmallow Fluff, egg whites, water, sugar, cream of tartar, and salt. Use a hand mixer on high speed to beat until soft peaks form. Remove from the heat and continue beating until stiff. Beat in the vanilla.

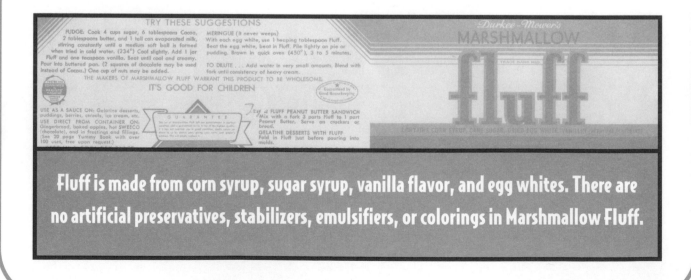

Fluff is made from corn syrup, sugar syrup, vanilla flavor, and egg whites. There are no artificial preservatives, stabilizers, emulsifiers, or colorings in Marshmallow Fluff.

Broiled Fluff Frosting

Makes enough to frost one 9-inch square cake

1 cup Marshmallow Fluff

¹⁄₃ cup unsalted butter or margarine, softened

1 cup sweetened flaked coconut

¹⁄₂ cup chopped walnuts

¹⁄₄ teaspoon salt

• In a mixing bowl, combine the Marshmallow Fluff, butter, coconut, walnuts, and salt. Spread over the top of a

  hot cake. Place under the broiler for about 2 minutes, or until golden brown.

Fluff-Chocolate Frosting

It's so smooth, rich, and creamy—it tastes like fudge.

Makes enough to fill and frost two 8- or 9-inch cake layers

3 ounces unsweetened chocolate

3/4 cup boiling water

1/2 cup sugar

3 tablespoons cornstarch

1/4 teaspoon salt

2 cups Marshmallow Fluff

2 tablespoons unsalted butter or margarine

1 1/2 teaspoons vanilla extract

- In a medium saucepan, combine the chocolate and water. Cook, stirring, over low heat until the chocolate melts. In a mixing bowl, thoroughly combine the sugar, cornstarch, and salt. Stir the sugar mixture into the melted chocolate. Bring to a boil and cook, stirring continuously, until smooth and thick. Remove from the heat and stir in the Marshmallow Fluff, butter, and vanilla. Continue to stir until the mixture has cooled, then use immediately.

Creamy Bittersweet Frosting

Makes enough to fill and frost two 8- or 9-inch cake layers

2 cups Marshmallow Fluff

3 ounces unsweetened chocolate, melted

3 large egg yolks

$1/4$ cup ($1/2$ stick) unsalted butter or margarine, softened

1 teaspoon vanilla extract

$2^1/2$ cups sifted confectioners' sugar

- In a mixing bowl, combine the Marshmallow Fluff, melted chocolate, egg yolks, butter, and vanilla. Add the confectioners' sugar and beat until smooth and fluffy.

Fluff may look the same as generic marshmallow creme, but appearances can be deceiving. Fluff is made by a batch-whipping process (the same way it's always been made). Creme is whipped in a continuous mixing process. The texture of real Fluff is just so much more enjoyable, Fluff fans know that there is no comparison.

Have you ever wondered what
the eight-digit code
on the Fluff cap means?
It tells the year, day,
and time of manufacture.
The first number is the year,
the next three numbers
are the Julian date (1–365),
and the last four are the
military time of manufacture.
A code of 41961350 shows
a date of July 15, 2004, 1:50 P.M.

Mocha Frosting

Makes enough to fill and frost two 8-inch cake layers

$\frac{1}{2}$ cup (1 stick) unsalted butter or margarine, softened

$\frac{1}{2}$ cup unsweetened cocoa

1 teaspoon vanilla extract

1 tablespoon Marshmallow Fluff

3 cups sifted confectioners' sugar

$\frac{1}{4}$ cup cold strong coffee

• In a mixing bowl with a mixer on high speed, beat the butter and cocoa until light and fluffy. Stir in the vanilla and Marshmallow Fluff and blend well. Add the confectioners' sugar, $\frac{1}{4}$ cup at a time, alternating with the coffee, stirring well after each addition.

Berry Frosting

Try substituting raspberry or strawberry Fluff.

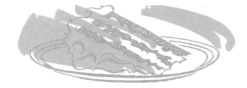

Makes enough to frost one 8-inch square cake

¹/₄ cup frozen strawberries or raspberries, thawed

2 tablespoons freshly squeezed lemon juice

1 tablespoon Marshmallow Fluff

About 2 cups sifted confectioners' sugar

• In a mixing bowl, combine the berries and lemon juice. Add the Marshmallow Fluff and blend well. Add the confectioners' sugar, ¹/₄ cup at a time, stirring well after each addition.

Fondant Frosting

Makes about 2 cups

6 tablespoons milk

2 tablespoons unsalted butter

¹/₂ cup Marshmallow Fluff

About 4 cups sifted confectioners' sugar

• In a medium saucepan over low heat, heat the milk until hot. Add the butter and stir until melted. Add the Marshmallow Fluff and stir until perfectly smooth. Add the confectioners' sugar, ¹/₄ cup at a time, stirring well after each addition until it reaches a good spreading consistency. When using the mixture for petits fours, add just enough sugar to make the frosting thin enough to pour but thick enough to cover the cakes.

A few More Fluff Delights

It turns out that more than just a few of America's top pastry chefs and cookbook authors are Marshmallow Fluff fanatics. The response was overwhelming when we asked them to contribute recipe ideas for using Fluff. These recipes are a bit more complex than the Durkee-Mower classics, but they're worth the extra effort.

Andy Schloss' Caramel Chipotle Popcorn Cakes

These are ingenious snacks—caramel sweet, lightly buttered, smoky hot. Because caramelizing sugar is difficult and slightly hazardous, this method streamlines the process by using Marshmallow Fluff. The technique for this recipe, adapted from a recipe in my cookbook *Almost from Scratch*, is similar to making marshmallow-crispy rice treats except that you cook the marshmallow mixture a little longer to caramelize its sugar, before you add the popcorn.—Andy Schloss

Makes about 24 cakes

11 cups salted popcorn (about ¼ cup unpopped kernels)

¾ cup (3 ounces) pecan pieces

1½ tablespoons butter

2 tablespoons water

1¾ cups Marshmallow Fluff

1 teaspoon ground chipotle pepper

Nonstick cooking spray

- In a large bowl, combine the popcorn and the pecans. In a heavy saucepan, combine the butter and water and bring to a boil. Stir in the Marshmallow Fluff and continue stirring and scraping until the mixture melts and browns lightly, about 2 minutes. Remove the pan from the heat and stir in the chipotle pepper. Scrape the mixture into the popcorn and mix until the popcorn and pecans are completely coated. Let sit for 1 minute.

- Scrape the popcorn mixture onto a cutting board. Spray your hands with the cooking spray and use them to form the mixture into a tightly packed log, about 16 inches long. Allow to set until firm, about 15 minutes. To serve, cut into rounds about ½ inch wide each.

Andrew Schloss, the president of the product development company Culinary Generations, Inc., is a former president of the International Association of Culinary Professionals (IACP) and the author of seven cookbooks, including *Almost from Scratch* (Simon & Schuster 2003) and *Fifty Ways to Cook Most Everything* (Simon & Schuster 1992).

Gale Gand's Chocolate and Fluff Shortbread Sandwiches

Because I have a 7-year-old, marshmallows tend to be one of the major food groups in my house, and roasting marshmallows is one of our favorite family activities. We always have a jar of Marshmallow Fluff in the cupboard for treats like eating it with bananas or, as my husband does, spreading it on chocolate chip cookies and gingersnaps. It's fun food.—Gale Gand

Makes 16 sandwiches

1 cup (2 sticks) unsalted butter, at room temperature

3/4 cup sugar

1 3/4 cups plus 2 tablespoons all-purpose flour

1/4 cup Dutch-processed cocoa powder

1/4 teaspoon salt

1 cup Marshmallow Fluff

- Preheat the oven to 375°F.

- Line an 8-inch square baking pan with foil or parchment paper.

- In the bowl of a mixer fitted with the paddle attachment, combine the butter and sugar and beat until smooth and creamy. Add the flour, cocoa powder, and salt and mix just until blended. Pat into the prepared pan in an even layer. With a fork, prick the surface all over to allow air to escape during baking. Bake for 20 to 25 minutes, rotating the pan halfway through the baking time.

- Cut up immediately into fingers 2 inches long by 1 inch wide and let them cool completely. Spread half of the fingers with Marshmallow Fluff and top with the other half to make sandwiches.

Award-winning executive pastry chef and partner of TRU in Chicago, Gale Gand is the coauthor of *American Brasserie* (Wiley 1997) and the author of *Butter Sugar Flour Eggs* (Clarkson Potter 1999), *Gale Gand's Just a Bite* (Clarkson Potter 2001), and *Gale Gand's Short and Sweet* (Clarkson Potter 2004). She is also the host of her own Food Network show, *Sweet Dreams*.

Carole Bloom's White Delight

This easy-to-make cake is loved by everyone. An angel food cake is frosted with Marshmallow Fluff that is mixed with shredded sweetened coconut. By using a store-bought angel food cake, this recipe can be assembled on the spur of the moment and is the perfect dessert to make when unexpected guests arrive.—Carole Bloom

Serves 12 to 14

3³⁄₄ cups Marshmallow Fluff

¹⁄₄ cup water

1 tablespoon vanilla extract

4 cups shredded sweetened coconut

One 9-inch round angel food cake

- Place the Marshmallow Fluff in a large mixing bowl or in the bowl of an electric stand mixer. Using the paddle attachment or a hand-held mixer, beat the Fluff lightly. Add the water and vanilla and beat until smooth, about a minute. Stop a couple of times and scrape down the bottom and sides of the bowl with a rubber spatula. Add the coconut and beat on medium speed until well blended.

- Place the cake onto a serving plate. Arrange strips of waxed paper around the bottom of the cake to keep the plate clean while applying the frosting. Using a flexible spatula, spread the top of the cake with ¹⁄₃ of the Fluff mixture. Spread the sides of the cake with the remaining mixture. Remove the waxed paper strips. Cut the cake into serving pieces. Store the cake tented with aluminum foil or in a covered cake dish at room temperature for up to 2 days.

Carole Bloom, CCP, is the author of seven dessert cookbooks. Her latest books are *Chocolate Lover's Cookbook for Dummies* (Wiley 2002), *Cookies for Dummies* (Wiley 2001), and the revised and updated edition of *Truffles, Candies, and Confections: Elegant Candymaking in the Home* (Ten Speed Press 2004).

Sally Sampson's
Fluff Rocky Road Bars

These bars, adapted from a recipe in *The Bake Sale Cookbook*, are not for the faint of heart, but they definitely have a place on the bake sale table. My 6-year-old daughter, Lauren, cut herself an average-size piece and after eating a fourth of it asked if it would be okay if she took a little break.—Sally Sampson

Makes 36 to 48 bars

For the First Layer:

1/2 cup (1 stick) unsalted butter

1 ounce unsweetened chocolate

1 cup sugar

2 large eggs, at room temperature

1 teaspoon vanilla extract

1 cup all-purpose flour

1/2 to 1 cup coarsely chopped toasted walnuts, pecans, or peanuts

1 teaspoon baking powder

For the Second Layer:

6 ounces cream cheese, at room temperature

1/4 cup (1/2 stick) unsalted butter, at room temperature

1 large egg, at room temperature

1/2 teaspoon vanilla extract

1/2 cup sugar

2 tablespoons all-purpose flour

1/4 cup toasted walnuts, pecans, or peanuts

1 cup (6 ounces) semisweet chocolate chips

One 7 1/2-ounce jar Marshmallow Fluff

For the Frosting:

1/4 cup (1/2 stick) unsalted butter

1 ounce unsweetened chocolate

2 ounces cream cheese

1/4 cup whole milk

1 cup confectioners' sugar

1 teaspoon vanilla extract

- Preheat the oven to 350°F.

- Lightly grease and flour a 13 x 9-inch baking pan.

- To prepare the first layer, place the butter and chocolate in a small saucepan and cook, stirring, over the lowest possible heat until the chocolate is almost completely melted. Turn off the heat, add the sugar, eggs, and vanilla and mix well. Mix in the flour, nuts, and baking powder until just combined. Press into the prepared pan and set aside.

- To prepare the second layer, in the bowl of a mixer fitted with the paddle attachment, combine the cream cheese, butter, egg, vanilla, sugar, and flour and mix until smooth and fluffy. Scrape down the sides of the bowl, add the nuts, mix to combine, and spread over the first layer. Sprinkle with the chocolate chips and bake in the oven until slightly golden on the edges, 20 to 25 minutes.

- Remove from the oven and very gently spread the Marshmallow Fluff over the top. Return to the oven and bake for about 5 minutes more.

- To prepare the frosting, place the butter and chocolate in a small saucepan and cook, stirring, over the lowest possible heat until the chocolate is almost completely melted. Add the cream cheese and milk and mix until smooth. Add the confectioners' sugar and vanilla and mix until smooth. Immediately pour the frosting over the Fluff and briefly swirl together for a marbleized look. Cool in the pan, then cover and refrigerate before cutting into bars.

Sally Sampson, a contributor to magazines such as *Self*, *Bon Appétit*, and *Food & Wine*, is the author of the James Beard Award—nominated *The $50 Dinner Party* (Fireside 2000), *Party Nuts* (Harvard Common Press 2002), and *Party Dips* (Harvard Common Press 2004) and the coauthor of several other cookbooks, including *The Olives Table* (Simon & Schuster 1997) and *The Figs Table* (Simon & Schuster 1998).

Carolyn Beth Weil's
Quick Fluff Buttercream

I was preparing to teach a basic baking class with a classic French buttercream on the menu. I kept thinking there was nothing basic about that recipe when I remembered a passing comment another author/baker made to me: "Have you tried making a quick buttercream with Fluff as the base?" I hadn't taken the comment seriously then, but when faced with trying to make a complicated recipe simple, I started experimenting with Fluff buttercream. It was so easy and tasty I brought the recipe to class. Try it on any of your favorite cakes; the coffee flavor is great with a chocolate cake, the lemon on a poppy seed cake, and the chocolate just about anywhere—even cupcakes.—Carolyn Beth Weil

Makes enough for one 2-layer 8-inch cake

One 7$\frac{1}{2}$-ounce jar Marshmallow Fluff

1$\frac{1}{2}$ cups (3 sticks) unsalted butter, at room temperature

• Soften the Marshmallow Fluff for 30 seconds (based on a 600-watt oven) in the microwave. Scrape the entire contents of the jar into a medium bowl. With an electric mixer on high, whip the Fluff until smooth. Add the butter in small pieces and whip until smooth. Scrape the bowl well and whip until smooth. Use immediately, or mix in one of the flavorings listed (opposite page) just until fully incorporated.

Variations:

Chocolate:

Melt 5 ounces of bittersweet chocolate and let stand until barely warm. Mix into the buttercream as directed.

White Chocolate:

Melt 6 ounces of white chocolate and let stand until barely warm. Mix into the buttercream as directed.

Coffee:

Dissolve 1 to 2 tablespoons instant coffee powder in 1 tablespoon hot water until dissolved. Mix into the buttercream as directed.

Orange:

Combine 2 teaspoons freshly grated orange zest and 1 to 3 drops orange oil (or $\frac{1}{4}$ teaspoon orange extract). Mix into the buttercream as directed.

Carolyn Beth Weil has spent more than thirty years in the food industry in California. She worked in three-star restaurants and owned a bakery for a decade but now strives to make baking approachable to the home cook through teaching and writing. She is a contributor to *The Baker's Dozen Cookbook*, *Fine Cooking* magazine, and *The Washington Post*. Her latest book, *Pie and Tart*, for the Williams-Sonoma Collection was published in March 2003. She is now writing *Fruit Desserts*, due out in 2005.

Dede Wilson's
Marshmallow Black Bottom Pie

Homemade marshmallows are making the rounds, often in s'mores or as a topping for hot chocolate. They are an all-American confection and—in the guise of a fluffy topping—match perfectly with this old-fashioned black bottom pie, itself an example of the retro/diner desserts that have made a comeback.—Dede Wilson

Serves 6 to 8

One unbaked 9-inch deep dish piecrust

For the Filling:

½ cup sugar

¼ cup cornstarch

1 tablespoon Dutch-processed cocoa powder

Pinch of salt

4 large egg yolks

2 cups whole milk

½ cup heavy whipping cream

5 ounces bittersweet chocolate, finely chopped

1 tablespoon unsalted butter

1 teaspoon vanilla extract

One recipe Fluff Meringue (see recipe, page 35)

- Preheat the oven to 375°F.

- Line the piecrust with foil and pie weights (or dry beans) and bake for 20 minutes. Remove the foil and weights and bake for 10 minutes more. Place on a wire rack to cool.

- As soon as the pie shell is removed from the oven, prepare the filling. Place the sugar, cornstarch, cocoa, and salt in a small nonreactive saucepan and whisk to blend. Whisk in the egg yolks, then immediately whisk in the milk and cream. Place over medium heat, whisking frequently, until it comes to a simmer. Simmer for 1 minute, whisking constantly. The mixture should be thickened—drawing a spoon along the bottom of the saucepan should leave a trail. Remove from the heat and whisk in the chocolate until combined, then quickly whisk in the butter and vanilla.

- Immediately pour into the still-warm baked pie shell. Cool on the wire rack for 10 minutes, then prepare the Fluff Meringue. (Or the pie may be held at this point for most of the day.)

- Preheat the broiler. Scrape the Fluff Meringue onto the pie, using a rubber spatula to make decorative peaks. Place the pie under the broiler for 1 to 2 minutes, or until the topping is lightly browned. Let sit 15 minutes or for up to 2 hours before serving.

Dede Wilson, a contributing editor to *Bon Appétit* magazine as well as to *Pastry Art & Design* magazine, is the host of the PBS show *Seasonings with Dede Wilson* and makes regular appearances on programs such as the *Today* show and *The View*. She is also the author of several books, including *The Wedding Cake Book* (Wiley 1997), *Christmas Cooking for Dummies* (Hungry Minds 2001), and *A Baker's Field Guide to Christmas Cookies* (Harvard Common Press 2003).

Dede Wilson's Pumpkin 'n' Fluff Streusel Snack Cake

This ultra-moist cake has pumpkin and sour cream in the batter with a ribbon of Fluff in the middle. It is lightly spiced with cinnamon, ginger, and cardamom along with a crunchy and sweet brown sugar–walnut streusel.

—Dede Wilson

Serves 16

For the Streusel:

1/4 cup chopped walnuts

2 tablespoons firmly packed light brown sugar

1 teaspoon ground cinnamon

For the Cake:

2 cups all-purpose flour

1 teaspoon baking powder

1 teaspoon baking soda

1/2 teaspoon ground cardamom

1/4 teaspoon ground cinnamon

1/4 teaspoon ground ginger

1/4 teaspoon salt

1 cup (2 sticks) unsalted butter, at room temperature,

   cut into pieces

1 cup firmly packed light brown sugar

1/2 cup canned pumpkin puree

1 teaspoon vanilla extract

2 large eggs

3/4 cup full-fat sour cream

1 cup Marshmallow Fluff

- Preheat the oven to 325°F.

- Grease a 9-inch square baking pan and dust with flour.

108

- To prepare the streusel, in a small bowl, toss together the walnuts, brown sugar, and cinnamon; set aside.

- To prepare the cake, in a mixing bowl, stir together the flour, baking powder, baking soda, cardamom, cinnamon, ginger, and salt to aerate and combine. Set aside. In the bowl of a stand mixer with the flat paddle attachment on medium speed, beat the butter until creamy, about 2 minutes. Add the brown sugar and beat until light and fluffy, about 2 minutes more. Beat in the pumpkin puree and vanilla. The mixture might look curdled, which is fine. Beat in the eggs one at a time until combined. Add the flour mixture and sour cream alternately on low speed just until combined.

- Spread half of the batter in the bottom of the baking pan, using a small offset spatula to create a smooth, even layer. Sprinkle with half of the streusel. Drop the Marshmallow Fluff in dollops all over the cake's surface. Top with the remaining cake batter, again using an offset spatula to spread evenly. Don't worry if a few pockets of Fluff peak out. Top with the remaining streusel.

- Bake for 50 to 60 minutes, or until an inserted toothpick comes out clean, rotating the pan once during the baking time. Place the pan on a wire rack to cool before cutting into squares. This is wonderful served warm. The cake will keep for 3 days at room temperature in an airtight container.

Dede Wilson, a contributing editor to *Bon Appétit* magazine as well as to *Pastry Art & Design* magazine, is the host of the PBS show *Seasonings with Dede Wilson* and makes regular appearances on programs such as the *Today* show and *The View*. She is also the author of several books, including *The Wedding Cake Book* (Wiley 1997), *Christmas Cooking for Dummies* (Hungry Minds 2001), and *A Baker's Field Guide to Christmas Cookies* (Harvard Common Press 2003).

Lauren Chattman's
Mocha-Almond Fudge

I must have been about 10 years old when I first made fudge with Marshmallow Fluff. This secret ingredient eliminates the need for tricky heating and cooling steps taken to make traditional fudge. This recipe, taken from my upcoming cookbook, *Icebox Desserts* (Harvard Common Press 2004), is grown-up fudge, but so easy to make that even a kid could do it. The addition of espresso powder, cinnamon, and almonds to my basic fudge recipe yields this terrific confection.—Lauren Chattman

Makes 16 squares, about 2 pounds

1 cup sugar

One 7$^1/_2$-ounce jar Marshmallow Fluff

$^2/_3$ cup evaporated milk

6 tablespoons unsalted butter

1 tablespoon instant espresso powder

$^1/_4$ teaspoon ground cinnamon

$^1/_4$ teaspoon salt

14 ounces bittersweet chocolate, finely chopped

2$^1/_2$ cups almonds, coarsely chopped

1 teaspoon vanilla extract

• Line an 8-inch square baking pan with heavy-duty aluminum foil, making sure that the foil is tucked into all the corners and that there is at least 1 inch overhanging the top of the pan on all sides.

• Combine the sugar, Marshmallow Fluff, evaporated milk, butter, espresso powder, cinnamon, and salt in a medium saucepan. Cook over medium heat, stirring frequently, until it comes to a boil. Boil for 5 minutes, stirring constantly.

• Remove from the heat and stir in the chocolate until smooth. Stir in the nuts and vanilla. Scrape into the prepared pan and smooth with a spatula. Refrigerate until firm, about 2 hours.

Lauren Chattman, a former pastry chef and the author of *Mom's Big Book of Baking* (Harvard Common Press 2001) and *Icebox Pies* (Harvard Common Press 2002), is a contributor to publications including *Bon Appétit*, *Cook's Illustrated*, and *The New York Times*.

Lora Brody's Classic Hot Chocolate

This classic concoction gives you a brown and white mustache—a really good excuse to lick your lips. I love the way the Fluff melts into a sweet puddle through which your spoon gets to slip on its way to chocolate Nirvana. Use bittersweet chocolate to counterbalance the sweetness of the topping.—Lora Brody

Serves 6

1 cup heavy whipping cream

8 ounces bittersweet chocolate, coarsely chopped

3 cups whole milk

¾ cup Marshmallow Fluff

- Heat the heavy cream in a medium saucepan set over medium heat until tiny bubbles form around the edges of the pan. Remove the pan from the heat and add the chocolate. Stir until the chocolate melts. Divide this mixture among 6 mugs. Heat the milk in the same saucepan until small bubbles appear around the edges but before a skin starts to form on top. Divide the milk among the mugs. Stir the hot chocolate and serve immediately with a generous dollop of Marshmallow Fluff.

Lora Brody is the author of more than twenty cookbooks. Her latest are *The Cape Cod Table* (Chronicle Books 2003) and *Chocolate American Style* (Clarkson Potter 2004).

Tish Boyle's Black and White Chocolate Marshmallow Brownies

The intensity of these dense chocolate brownies is complemented by the addition of a voluptuous marshmallow topping, set off by a drizzle of more chocolate. Their stunning appearance is bound to be the talk of the bake sale.—Tish Boyle

Makes 20 brownies

$1/2$ cup (1 stick) unsalted butter, cut into tablespoons

9 ounces semisweet or bittersweet chocolate, coarsely chopped

1 ounce unsweetened chocolate, coarsely chopped

$3/4$ cup sugar

3 large eggs

$1^1/2$ teaspoons vanilla extract

$1/2$ cup all-purpose flour

$1/8$ teaspoon salt

$3/4$ cup pecans, coarsely chopped

1 cup Marshmallow Fluff

1 ounce semisweet or bittersweet chocolate, melted

- Position a rack in the center of the oven and preheat to 325°F.

- Line a 9-inch square baking pan with aluminum foil so that the foil extends 2 inches beyond two opposite sides of the pan. Lightly grease the bottom and sides of the foil-lined pan.

- In the top of a double boiler over barely simmering water, heat the butter with the semisweet and unsweetened chocolates, stirring occasionally, until melted and smooth. Transfer the mixture to a large bowl and stir in the sugar. Using a wooden spoon, mix in the eggs, one at a time, incorporating well before the next addition. Mix in the vanilla. Add the flour and salt and mix vigorously until the mixture pulls away from the side of the bowl. Stir in the pecans. Scrape the batter into the prepared pan and smooth the top with a rubber spatula. Bake the brownies for 30 to 35 minutes, or until a cake tester inserted in the center of the brownies comes out with a few moist crumbs clinging to it. Do not overbake. Place the pan on a wire rack.

• Spoon the Marshmallow Fluff, in 4 large dollops, over the hot brownies. Using a small offset metal spatula, spread the Fluff over the brownies in a smooth, even layer, covering the top completely. Let the brownies cool for 45 minutes.

• To garnish the brownies, scrape the melted chocolate into a small, sealable plastic bag. Seal the bag and snip a tiny hole in the corner. Drizzle the chocolate in a diagonal zigzag pattern over the marshmallow topping. Let the brownies cool for another 30 minutes before serving. Cut into 20 rectangles and store in an airtight container.

Tish Boyle is the food editor of *Chocolatier* and *Pastry Art & Design* magazines. She is the coauthor of *Grand Finales: The Art of the Plated Dessert* (John Wiley & Sons 1996) and the author of *Diner Desserts* (Chronicle Books 2000) and *The Good Cookie* (John Wiley & Sons 2002).

Dorie Greenspan's Fluff-filled Chocolate Madeleines

As if these adorable chocolate-dipped madeleines aren't already tempting enough, Dorie suggests squiggling a little Fluff on top of each madeleine for a decorative touch.

Makes 12 Madeleines

For the Madeleines:

$^2/_3$ cup all-purpose flour

$^1/_4$ cup Dutch-processed cocoa powder

$^1/_2$ teaspoon double acting baking powder

Pinch of salt

2 large eggs, at room temperature

$^1/_2$ cup sugar

$^1/_2$ teaspoon vanilla extract

6 tablespoons unsalted butter, melted and cooled

Marshmallow Fluff, for filling

For the Dip (optional, but yummy):

4 ounces bittersweet chocolate, finely chopped

$^1/_2$ cup heavy whipping cream

$1^1/_2$ tablespoons unsalted butter, at room temperature

• In a mixing bowl, sift the flour, cocoa, baking powder, and salt together and set aside. In another bowl, beat the eggs and sugar together until pale and slightly thickened, about 3 minutes. Beat in the vanilla. With a large rubber spatula, gently fold in the sifted dry ingredients, followed by the melted butter. Put a piece of plastic wrap directly against the surface of the batter and chill the batter for at least 3 hours or overnight.

- Center a rack in the oven and preheat to 400°F. Generously butter the molds in a madeleine pan, dust with flour, and tap out the excess. (Butter and flour the pan even if it is nonstick; you can skip this step if you are using silicone pans.) Place the pan on a rimmed baking sheet for easier transporting.

- Divide the batter among the 12 madeleine shells and slide the baking pan into the oven. Immediately lower the oven temperature to 350°F and bake for 13 to 15 minutes, or until they feel springy to the touch. Remove the pan from the oven and rap one side of the madeleine pan against the counter—the plump little cakes should come tumbling out. (Pry any reluctant cookies out with a blunt knife.) Cool to room temperature on a rack.

- Put some Marshmallow Fluff in a small sealable plastic bag, seal the bag, and snip off the tip of one corner. Use a small knife to cut a little cone of cookie out of the rounded side of each madeleine and squeeze some Fluff into each hole; plug with the cone.

- To make the dip, put the chocolate in a small heatproof bowl. Bring the heavy cream to a full boil, then pour over the chocolate. Wait 1 minute before gently whisking the cream into the chocolate. Start at the center and slowly work your way out in concentric circles until smooth and shiny. Gently whisk in the butter.

- Line a small baking sheet with waxed paper. Holding by the narrow end, dip each madeleine into the chocolate. Lift the cookie up, let the excess chocolate drip back into the bowl, and place the cookie, plain side down, on the waxed paper. Slide the sheet into the refrigerator to set the glaze, about 15 minutes. Eat within 1 day. Leftover dip can be covered and refrigerated for 1 week or frozen for up to 1 month.

Dorie Greenspan is the award-winning author of eight cookbooks, among them *Baking with Julia* (William Morrow 1996), the book that accompanies Julia Child's PBS series, and *Paris Sweets: Great Desserts from the City's Best Pastry Shops* (Broadway Books 2002). A contributing editor at *Bon Appétit* magazine, Dorie is working on a new book, *Baking, From My Home to Yours* (Houghton Mifflin 2006).

Nicole Kaplan's Chocolate Cupcakes with Cream Filling

No day is complete without a little bit of Fluff. I never liked jelly as a kid, and I only ate my peanut butter one way, the Fluffernutter. It wasn't until I was much older that I realized Fluff could be so versatile. I only wish it came in bigger jars.—Nicole Kaplan

Makes 1 dozen cupcakes

For the Cupcakes:

1/2 cup plus 2 tablespoons cake flour

1/3 cup unsweetened Dutch-process cocoa powder

1/2 teaspoon baking powder

1/4 teaspoon baking soda

Pinch of salt

2 large eggs, separated

1/3 cup canola oil

1/2 cup plus 2 tablespoons sugar

2 tablespoons water

For the Filling:

6 tablespoons unsalted butter, softened

1 1/2 cups confectioners' sugar

3/4 cup Marshmallow Fluff

1 1/2 tablespoons plus 1 teaspoon heavy whipping cream

For the Frosting:

1/4 cup heavy whipping cream

4 ounces bittersweet chocolate, finely chopped

1 tablespoon unsalted butter, softened

- To prepare the cupcakes: Preheat the oven to 350°F. Coat a 12-cup nonstick muffin pan with nonstick cooking spray.

- In a medium bowl, sift the flour and cocoa with the baking powder, baking soda, and salt. In another bowl, using an electric mixer, beat the egg yolks with the canola oil, 1/2 cup of the sugar, and the water. Beat in the dry ingredients at low speed until smooth.

- In a clean bowl, using clean beaters, beat the egg whites at high speed until soft peaks form. Add the remaining 2 tablespoons of sugar and beat until stiff and glossy. Beat one-fourth of the whites into the batter, then fold in the remaining whites until no streaks remain. Spoon the batter into the muffin cups, filling them halfway. Bake for 15 minutes, or until the cupcakes are springy when touched. Let the cupcakes cool for 5 minutes, then turn them out onto a wire rack to cool completely.

- To prepare the filling: In a medium bowl, beat the butter with the confectioners' sugar, Marshmallow Fluff, and 1½ tablespoons of the heavy cream at medium speed until fluffy. Transfer all but ½ cup of the filling to a pastry bag fitted with a ¼-inch plain round tip. Beat the remaining 1 teaspoon of cream into the remaining ½ cup of filling and reserve.

- Line a large baking sheet with waxed paper. Insert the tip of the pastry bag about ½ inch deep into the bottom of each cupcake and squeeze lightly to fill with cream. Set the cupcakes on the sheet.

- To make the frosting: Heat the cream in a small saucepan until steaming. Add the chocolate and let stand for 5 minutes. Add the butter and stir until smooth. Spread the top of each cupcake with the frosting. Spoon the reserved filling into a pastry bag fitted with a very small plain tip and pipe decorative swirls on each cupcake. Refrigerate the cupcakes for at least 10 minutes to set the frosting.

Named one of *Pastry Art & Design* magazine's Top Ten Pastry Chefs in America for 2003, Nicole Kaplan trained at Peter Kump's New York Cooking School, where she graduated with a Blue Ribbon in 1997. Since then, she has worked at popular New York restaurants, including Sign of the Dove, Osteria del Circo and, since 2000, as pastry chef at Eleven Madison Park.

Bruce Weinstein & Mark Scarbrough's
Marshmallow Fluff Brownies

While they bake, the batter puffs up then collapses down into thin, fudgy brownies. With an almost candy bar–like quality (reminiscent of Three Musketeers bars), they're the perfect way to satisfy the cookie and candy lover in your life—in one treat.—B.W. and M.S.

Makes twenty-four 2¼ x 2¼-inch brownies

¾ cup all-purpose flour

¼ cup cocoa powder, sifted

1 teaspoon baking powder

½ teaspoon salt

10 tablespoons unsalted butter, at room temperature

1 cup sugar

1 large egg, at room temperature

1 large egg yolk, at room temperature

1 teaspoon vanilla extract

One 7½-ounce jar Marshmallow Fluff

3 ounces unsweetened chocolate, melted and cooled

- Position the rack in the middle of the oven. Preheat the oven to 350°F.

- Grease and flour a 13 x 9-inch baking pan and set aside.

- In a medium bowl, stir together the flour, cocoa, baking powder, and salt until well combined. Set aside.

- In a large bowl with an electric mixer on medium speed, beat the butter and sugar until pale yellow and thick.

- Beat in the egg and egg yolk until thoroughly incorporated. Beat for 1 minute more, then add the vanilla and

Marshmallow Fluff. Beat on medium-high speed until the mixture is smooth and uniform. Add the melted chocolate and beat on low speed until it is evenly blended.

• With a rubber spatula or wooden spoon, fold in the flour mixture just until the dry ingredients are incorporated. Do not overmix. Spread the batter into the prepared pan.

• Bake for 30 to 35 minutes, or until the top is set but soft. It is okay if a toothpick inserted in the center has a bit of chocolate attached. Set the pan on a wire rack and cool for at least 2 hours before cutting. Cut the brownies into 24 pieces while still in the pan.

Bruce Weinstein and Mark Scarbrough are the top-selling coauthors of cookbooks such as *The Ultimate Ice Cream Cookbook* (William Morrow 1999), *The Ultimate Brownie Cookbook* (William Morrow 2002), and *The Ultimate Potato Cookbook* (William Morrow 2002). They are also regular contributors to publications including *Wine Spectator*, *The New York Times*, *Weight Watchers*, *Cooking Light*, *Fine Cooking*, and *Gourmet*. Bruce makes frequent appearances on *Home Matters* and QVC.

Lee Zalben's Peanut Butter Banana Ring

Perfect with a cup of coffee or a glass of milk. The addition of Marshmallow Fluff in the recipe makes this cake extra moist and delicious. Any natural, unsweetened peanut butter will do, but I highly recommend using my own brand, Peanut Butter & Co. Smooth Operator peanut butter. It's available in specialty food stores and better supermarkets across the country or online at www.ilovepeanutbutter.com.—Lee Zalben

Serves 10 to 12

2 large, very ripe bananas

2 cups (16 ounces) natural, unsweetened smooth peanut butter

$^1/_4$ cup ($^1/_2$ stick) unsalted butter, softened

1 tablespoon vanilla extract

1 cup firmly packed light brown sugar

One 7$^1/_2$-ounce jar Marshmallow Fluff

$^3/_4$ cup all-purpose unbleached flour

1 teaspoon ground cinnamon

$^1/_2$ teaspoon baking powder

$^1/_2$ teaspoon baking soda

$^3/_4$ cup egg whites (about 6 large egg whites)

1 cup confectioners' sugar

2 tablespoons water

• Preheat the oven to 325°F.

• Grease and flour a 10-inch tube pan and set aside.

- In a large bowl, combine the bananas, peanut butter, butter, and vanilla extract. Beat with an electric mixer until almost smooth. Add the brown sugar and continue to mix until the sugar is incorporated. Add the Marshmallow Fluff, reserving 2 heaping tablespoons in a small bowl to make the glaze. Mix until the Fluff is incorporated.

- In a separate bowl, sift together the flour, cinnamon, baking powder, and baking soda. Add the dry ingredients to the batter and mix just until incorporated.

- In a separate clean bowl and with immaculately clean and dry beaters, whip the egg whites until they form stiff peaks. With a rubber spatula, gently fold the egg whites into the cake batter and then spoon into the prepared cake pan. Bake for 50 minutes, or until an inserted knife comes out clean. Let the cake cool in the pan, then turn out to glaze.

- To make the glaze, in a small bowl, combine the confectioners' sugar and water and stir until all of the sugar is dissolved. Add the 2 tablespoons of reserved Fluff and stir until well incorporated. When the cake is cooled, drizzle the glaze over the cake. Allow to set for 1 hour before serving.

Lee Zalben, also known as "The Peanut Butter Guy," is the founder and president of the Peanut Butter & Co. sandwich shop in New York City's Greenwich Village. The shop, which opened in 1998, serves nothing but peanut butter sandwiches and desserts. Lee dreamed up the idea during late-night study breaks with his friends while a student at Vassar College. After working for several years in advertising after graduation, Lee opened the unique shop, whose menu features six different kinds freshly ground all-natural peanut butter.

Duane Winfield's Fluff and Nutella Sandwich

My good friend Duane Winfield proposed this clever combination, a variation on the Fluffernutter theme. It turns out he was onto something really delicious. Nutella and Fluff is a match made in Heaven. Not only is it tempting as a sandwich, but it's also fantastic when served, sans the bread, with fresh fruit like bananas or apple wedges for dipping.—J.S.

Serves 1

Nutella

2 slices sandwich bread

Marshmallow Fluff

• Spread one slice of the bread with Nutella. Top with a generous layer of Marshmallow Fluff. Top with the other slice of bread and slice.

Duane Winfield is a still-life photographer who specializes in food photography. His photography has appeared in such books as *Sally Sampson's Party Nuts* (Harvard Common Press 2002), *The El Paso Chile Company Margarita Cookbook* (William Morrow 1999), and *Carole Walter's Great Cookies* (Clarkson Potter 2003).

Stonewall Kitchen Crispy Rice Treat Sandwiches

I grew up in Massachusetts, not far from the Fluff factory in Lynn, and I can't remember ever not having Fluff in the house when I was a child. We serve these "gourmet" crispy rice treats, made with our own Bittersweet Chocolate Sauce, in our café in York, Maine.—Jonathan King

Makes twenty-four 2-inch squares

¼ cup (½ stick) unsalted butter

One 7½-ounce jar Marshmallow Fluff

1 tablespoon vanilla extract

Pinch of salt

8 cups crispy rice cereal

One 12-ounce jar Stonewall Kitchen Bittersweet Chocolate Sauce

- Grease a 13 x 9-inch baking pan and set aside.
- In a heavy-bottomed saucepan over low heat, melt the butter. Add the Marshmallow Fluff, vanilla, and salt and cook over medium-high heat, stirring, until the mixture starts to bubble around the edges of the pan, about 5 minutes. Remove from the heat and add the crispy rice cereal. Stir until combined. Using a buttered spatula or waxed paper, press the mixture evenly into the baking pan. Cool completely.
- Cut into 2-inch squares (or whatever size desired). Spread half of the squares with the Bittersweet Chocolate Sauce, then place another square on top to make a sandwich and serve.

Jonathan King and Jim Stott founded Stonewall Kitchen in 1991 in York, Maine. Today their line of award-winning specialty foods can be found in gourmet shops and gifts stores across the country. They are the authors of *The Stonewall Kitchen Cookbook* (William Morrow 2001).

King Arthur Flour's
Midnight Mocha Madness

When you've got to have a hit of chocolate and coffee, this is where to go! These easy-to-make, one-bowl, stir-together cookies taste like rich hot chocolate with lots of Marshmallow Fluff on top, all wrapped into a warm cookie! They are rich with bittersweet chocolate, cocoa, and a hint of coffee. Leave your electric mixer in the cabinet and just stir the ingredients together.—King Arthur Flour

Makes 2½ dozen cookies

1½ cups (9 ounces) semisweet chocolate chips, or chopped bittersweet or semisweet chocolate

6 tablespoons (¾ stick) unsalted butter

⅓ cup cocoa (natural or Dutch-process)

¼ cup sugar

¼ teaspoon salt

1 teaspoon espresso powder or instant coffee (optional)

One 7½-ounce jar Marshmallow Fluff

1 cup unbleached all-purpose flour

½ teaspoon baking powder

2 teaspoons vanilla extract

1 large egg

1 cup chopped pecans or walnuts (optional)

- Preheat the oven to 400°F.
- In the top of a double boiler or in a microwave, melt together the chocolate, butter, cocoa, sugar, salt, and espresso powder or instant coffee, if using. Stir occasionally until smooth. Remove from the heat and stir the

Marshmallow Fluff into the warm chocolate mixture. Stir in the flour, baking powder, vanilla, and egg. Mix until the batter comes together; it will seem dry at first, but within a minute or so it will come together. Stir in the nuts, if using.

- Drop the cookie dough by the heaping tablespoonful onto a parchment-lined or lightly greased baking sheet, leaving about 2 inches between each cookie. A cookie scoop or small ice cream scoop makes this task simple. To keep the cookies from spreading too much as they bake, refrigerate the dough for at least 15 minutes before baking.

- Bake the cookies for 11 to 14 minutes, until their tops puff up and look set. You want these baked all the way through, but just barely; additional baking will make them cake-like rather than chewy-gooey. If you press them with your finger, a print will remain even though they're done.

- Remove the cookies from the oven. These beauties are fragile when hot, so allow them to cool on the baking sheet for 5 minutes, then use a spatula to move them to a wire rack. The cookies will fall slightly as they cool.

King Arthur Flour was founded in 1790 and remains America's premier-quality flour company, supplying unbleached, unbromated flour to home bakers, professional chefs, and bakeries throughout America. King Arthur Flour's Norwich, Vermont, headquarters is home to a renowned bakery, school, and store. The company also offers fine tools, ingredients, and recipes through *The Baker's Catalogue*, America's premier home-baking resource.

Index